Well Read 1

SKILLS AND STRATEGIES FOR READING

Laurie Blass

SERIES CONSULTANTS

Mindy Pasternak | Elisaveta Wrangell

OXFORD
UNIVERSITY PRESS

198 Madison Avenue
New York, NY 10016 USA

Great Clarendon Street, Oxford OX2 6DP UK

Oxford University Press is a department of the University of Oxford.
It furthers the University's objective of excellence in research, scholarship,
and education by publishing worldwide in

Oxford New York

Auckland Cape Town Dar es Salaam Hong Kong Karachi
Kuala Lumpur Madrid Melbourne Mexico City Nairobi
New Delhi Shanghai Taipei Toronto

With offices in

Argentina Austria Brazil Chile Czech Republic France Greece
Guatemala Hungary Italy Japan Poland Portugal Singapore
South Korea Switzerland Thailand Turkey Ukraine Vietnam

OXFORD and OXFORD ENGLISH are registered trademarks of
Oxford University Press

Editorial Director: Sally Yagan
Senior Acquisitions Editor: Pietro Alongi
Editor: Phebe W. Szatmari
Editorial Assistant: Beverley Langevine
Art Director: Maj Hagsted
Senior Designer: Claudia Carlson
Art Editor: Robin Fadool
Production Manager: Shanta Persaud
Production Controller: Soniya Kulkarni

ISBN: 978 0 19 476100 0

Printed in Hong Kong

10 9 8 7 6 5 4 3 2 1

ACKNOWLEDGMENTS

Cover art: Claudia Carlson

The authors and publisher would like to acknowledge the following indi-
viduals for their invaluable input during the development of this series:
Macarena Aguilar, Cy-Fair College, TX; Sharon Allerson, East Los Angeles
College, CA; Susan Niemeyer, Los Angeles City College, CA; Elaine S. Paris,
Koc University, Istanbul, Turkey; Sylvia Cavazos Pena, University of Texas
at Brownsville, TX; Maggy Sami Saba, King Abdulaziz University, Jeddah,
Kingdom of Saudi Arabia; Stephanie Toland, North Side Learning Center,
MN; Jay Myoung Yu, Yonsei University at Wonju, Korea; Anthony Zak,
Universitas Sam Ratulangi, Manado, Indonesia.

Special thanks go to Barbara Rifkind for her support of the editorial team.

AUTHOR ACKNOWLEDGMENTS

Many thanks to Mindy Pasternak and Elisaveta Wrangell, the originators of
this series, for their inspiration and creativity. Heartfelt thanks also go to
Elizabeth Whalley for her invaluable contributions to the early stages of this
book. Finally, I am very grateful to Phebe Szatmari and Pietro Alongi, and the
Oxford University Press editorial and design staff for all their hard work on
this project.

Notes to the Teacher

Welcome to *Well Read*, a four-level series that teaches and reinforces crucial reading skills and vocabulary strategies step-by-step through a wide range of authentic texts that are meant to engage students' (and teachers') interest. *Well Read 1* is intended for students at the beginning level.

Each of the eight chapters in the book revolves around a central theme, but every text in a chapter approaches the theme from a different angle or level of formality. This provides multiple insights into the subject matter, while at the same time developing reading skills. Thus, students will be able to approach the theme with increasing fluency.

Well Read is designed so that all the activities, including reading, are broken up into smaller pieces, and each has specific goals so that all students, regardless of their individual level, can participate and succeed. The activities in the book support the approach that students do *not* have to understand every word of a text in order to understand its basic themes. Vocabulary strategies in each chapter allow students to feel more comfortable guessing the meanings of unfamiliar words or phrases based on their context.

Chapter Introduction

The opening page introduces the chapter's theme. Questions and photographs are designed to activate the students' prior knowledge, as well as stimulate some limited discussion before the previewing, reading, and post-reading activities.

Getting Started

This activity precedes each text or graphic component. It is designed to help students focus in on a more specific topic through reflection and discussion. It also introduces a small number of critical vocabulary words or phrases.

Active Previewing

Active Previewing asks students to read only brief and selected parts of the text, and then answer very simple questions that focus on this material. This activity encourages the notion that students do not have to understand each and every word of what they are reading. There is a strong emphasis on how to preview a wide range of genres, both academic and non-academic, including—but not limited to—newspaper articles, online texts, magazine articles, textbook articles, tables, charts, graphs, timelines, and graphics.

Reading and Recalling

The first reading activity asks students to read and recall. This approach is less daunting than being presented with an entire text, and it also allows the students to retain more. Recalling encourages students to be accountable for the material they read. While students build their short-term memories, they begin to process information more quickly and holistically. Perfect recall is never the goal.

Understanding the Text

After each text, students are presented with a two-part reading comprehension activity. The first part checks the students' comprehension of the most basic ideas expressed in the text, whereas the second part challenges the students to recall other key ideas and information.

Reading Skills

Among other essential skills, students are introduced to *Topic, Main Idea,* and *Supporting Details* in separate chapters, which allows them to practice and master each of these skills before progressing to the next. Earlier chapters present choices in a multiple choice fashion, whereas subsequent chapters require the students to write their own interpretations. The ability to think critically about the information that is presented in the text is a crucial part of being an active reader. Students are first taught to distinguish between facts and opinions, and later, inferences. In the final chapters of the textbook, students will be asked to find facts and opinions and to make inferences of their own.

Vocabulary Strategies

Students first learn that they can understand the general idea of a text without understanding every word; however, skipping words is not always an option, thus students are introduced to different strategies throughout the book that can help them determine the meanings of new vocabulary without using their dictionaries. All vocabulary activities use examples from the texts themselves, yet the vocabulary strategies taught can be applied universally to reading that students do outside class. Developing these strategies will allow students to become more autonomous readers.

Discussing the Issues

Every text ends with a series of questions that encourage students to express their opinions and ideas about the general subject discussed in the text. The questions are designed to be communicative in that they strike upon compelling issues raised in the text.

Putting It On Paper

Reading and writing are two skills that inherently go together. The writing activity complements the chapter texts, yet it is also designed to stand independently should the teacher decide not to read all of the chapter texts. Each *Putting It On Paper* activity offers two writing prompts; the teacher can allow students to choose between the prompts or can select one prompt for all students to use.

Taking It Online

Each *Taking It Online* activity guides the students through the steps necessary for conducting online research, based on the theme of the chapter. Teachers might opt to prescreen a select number of websites in advance, thus directing the students to more reliable and useful sites. *Taking It Online* finishes with a follow-up activity that enables the students to take their research one step further, in pairs or groups.

An Answer Key, a PowerPoint® Teaching Tool, and an ExamView Pro® Test Generator with customizable tests and quizzes are also available with each level of *Well Read* in the *Well Read Instructor's Pack*.

Contents

Welcome to *Well Read*

Well Read 1 is the first level in a four-level reading series that strategically develops students' reading skills, setting them up for success as critical thinkers.

There are eight chapters in *Well Read* and seven sections in each chapter: *Chapter Introduction, Text 1, Text 2, Text 3, Text 4, Putting It On Paper,* and *Taking It Online.*

Chapter Introduction

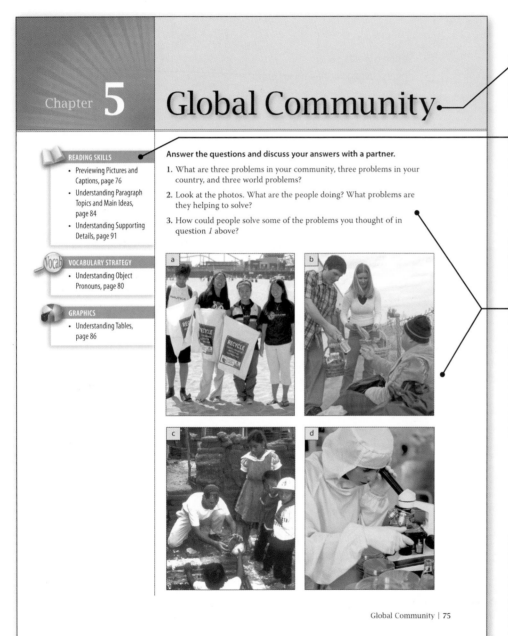

- The opening page of each chapter introduces the **chapter's theme.**

- *READING SKILLS, VOCABULARY STRATEGIES,* and *GRAPHICS* boxes outline the main features of the chapter and focus students' attention on what they will learn. Page references allow for easy access to a particular area of focus.

- **Questions** and **photographs** activate the students' prior knowledge of the theme, as well as stimulate a brief discussion. Pre-reading discussion serves to activate or create some knowledge of the subject.

> **NOTE**
> *Well Read* is designed so that a chapter can be taught in its entirety or individual chapter components can be selected, depending on the amount of time available.

Content shown within the chapter introduction image:

Chapter 5 — Global Community

READING SKILLS
- Previewing Pictures and Captions, page 76
- Understanding Paragraph Topics and Main Ideas, page 84
- Understanding Supporting Details, page 91

VOCABULARY STRATEGY
- Understanding Object Pronouns, page 80

GRAPHICS
- Understanding Tables, page 86

Answer the questions and discuss your answers with a partner.

1. What are three problems in your community, three problems in your country, and three world problems?

2. Look at the photos. What are the people doing? What problems are they helping to solve?

3. How could people solve some of the problems you thought of in question *1* above?

Global Community | 75

Text 1 | A Young Environmentalist

1 | Getting Started

A. Look at the chart about environmental problems. Add more problems. Rank them (number them in order) from most important to least important. Then write possible causes and solutions. Discuss your ideas with a partner.

Environmental problems	Rank	Possible cause(s)	Possible solution(s)
1. water pollution			
2. air pollution			
3. weather changes			
4. types of plants and animals disappearing			
5.			
6.			

B. Compare your chart with your classmates' charts. Do you agree or disagree on how to rank the problems? Do you agree or disagree on possible causes and solutions?

Getting Started

● Before each text, students **anticipate the more specific topic**—as opposed to the more generalized theme of the chapter.

● A small number of **critical vocabulary words or phrases** are introduced.

2 | Active Previewing

Preview the online interview below. Underline the important words in the title. Look at the pictures and captions. Make predictions. Then answer the following questions with a partner.

1. What is the topic of this text?
2. What kind of information will it probably have?

3 | Reading and Recalling

A. Read the text. Stop after each paragraph. Tell a partner one thing that you remember about it.

Active Previewing and Skimming

● Students are taught how to *actively* preview a wide range of genres, both academic and non-academic, including newspaper articles, online texts, magazine articles, textbook articles, and graphics (see *Graphics* on page xii).

2. How do you prepare for a job interview in your country? How might you prepare for a job interview in another country? Are there any differences?

3. How do you behave in a job interview in your country? How might you behave in a job interview in another country? Are there any differences?

B. Make a list of things that are important in a job interview (for example, appearance and work experience). Then rank the items in your list. Discuss your list with a partner.

READING SKILL Skimming

Skimming is moving your eyes over a text as you read quickly. You skim when you want to get a general idea about the information in the text but do not need to know all of the details.

Skimming is a good way to preview a text. It also helps you save time. For example, you skim when you want to see if the full text is something you want to read or if it will have the information you need.

To skim:

1. Read the title and any subtitles.
2. Read one or two paragraphs at the beginning.
3. Read the first and/or last sentence of the other paragraphs.
4. Look quickly at the other paragraphs. Read only a few words here and there. Notice names, places, dates and numbers, and words in bold or italic print.
5. Read the last paragraph.

● The skill of **skimming** a text for general meaning is also introduced in later chapters, at which point, there is no need to do a separate preview of a text.

Text 1, 2, and 4

The **texts** progress in length and level of difficulty in each chapter, and they are **authentic** in both presentation and content. Genres include: online texts, newspaper articles, magazine articles, and textbook articles, among others.

2 | Active Previewing

Preview the online interview below. <u>Underline</u> the important words in the title. Look at the pictures and captions. Make predictions. Then answer the following questions with a partner.

1. What is the topic of this text?
2. What kind of information will it probably have?

3 | Reading and Recalling

A. Read the text. Stop after each paragraph. Tell a partner one thing that you remember about it.

Interview with a Young Environmentalist[1]

by Yoonhee Ha, Assistant Editor, KSTR

1 Janine Licare is saving the world. She and her best friend started their own non-profit organization[2], Kids Saving the Rainforest in Costa Rica (KSTR). Today, the organization has many volunteers[3] around the world. Here's our interview with Janine.

2 **YH:** Janine, when you were only nine years old, you and a friend started Kids Saving the Rainforest, KSTR. How did you become interested in the rainforest?

JL: Well, we earned some money, but we didn't know what to do with it. Then we saw something terrible: People were cutting down all the trees around us in the rainforest. That helped us decide to try to save the rainforest.

Environmentalist Jani[ne] Kids Saving the Rainf[orest]

---
[1] **environmentalist:** a person who works to save the natural world
[2] **non-profit organization:** an organization with the goal of doing good work—no[t]
[3] **volunteers:** people who work without getting paid

Online texts

3 | Reading and Recalling

A. Read the text. Stop after each paragraph and tell a partner one thing that you remember about it.

What's Your Favorite Kind of Music?

BY MILES JONES

1 Today, our question is: What's your favorite kind of music?

2 **Helen, 45, college professor:** I love rock, especially oldies[1] such as the Beatles and the Rolling Stones. I don't like the pop[2] groups of today very much, though.

3 **Danielle, 13, student (Helen's daughter):** My favorite type of music is rock, too. I like the same stuff that my mom likes, but I like cool stuff, too. Like, I have Green Day and The White Stripes on my iPod®. Wanna listen?

4 **Marcus, 22, college student:** I like jazz and classical music. I'm an art major, and I listen to music while I work. Jazz and classical music inspire me[3]; they help me to think and to be creative.

5 **Pat, 33, musician:** I perform in the local symphony orchestra, so of course, I love classical music. I play the violin in the orchestra, but I play all kinds of stringed instruments. I love to listen to string ensembles[4] like the Eroica Trio.

6 **Rob, 21, waiter:** My favorite type of music is world music. I like music from lots of cultures. I like music from the Caribbean, especially reggae. I also like music from Latin America, like salsa and Asian fusion. That's traditional Asian music mixed with modern music.

7 **Chris, 27, computer graphics designer:** I like just about every kind of music. I love hip-hop and rap—that's what I listen to at work. The only kinds of music I absolutely do *not* like are country music and opera. I can't listen to them!

Newspaper articles

---
[1] **oldies:** older popular music—for example, from the 1960s, 1970s, or the 1980s
[2] **pop:** popular music
[3] **inspire me:** encourage me
[4] **ensembles:** small groups of musicians

B. Read the text again without stopping. Tell your partner two new pieces of information that you remember.

C. Work as a class or in small groups. Try to say as many things as you can about the text.

The Culture of Music | 57

A. Read the text. Stop after each paragraph. Tell a partner one thing that you remember about it.

The MacArthur "Genius" Grants[1]

1 Each year, the John D. and Catherine T. MacArthur Foundation gives prizes to very special people. These people are very smart and creative, so they are called "geniuses."

2 The winners receive $500, 000. The money comes with "no strings attached." For example, they can spend the money on anything they want.

3 People do not apply for the prizes. The foundation does not interview the people in order to choose the winners. Instead, the foundation organizes groups of nominators[2]. Nominators come from many different fields of study such as art, education, and science. They recommend the names of "geniuses" from their own fields. Then the foundation chooses the winners from the recommendations.

4 Here are some recent MacArthur Foundation winners:

5 **Gretchen Berland** is a doctor. She also is a filmmaker. She makes films about important problems in healthcare.

6 **James Carpenter** is a designer and an engineer. He designs buildings that use less energy and save money.

7 **Katherine Gottlieb** is CEO, or head, of a non-profit organization. Her organization is in Alaska. It gives excellent healthcare to poor Native Alaskans.

> The winners receive $500,000. The money comes with "no strings attached."

Gretchen Berland, doctor and filmmaker

[1] **grants:** amounts of money given for projects
[2] **nominators:** people who suggest possible participants in a contest

● Magazine articles

● Textbook articles

A New College Course: What Motivates[1] Altruism?

Students helping at a homeless shelter

1 Why do some people like to do good things such as helping others or saving the environment? They don't do these things for money. This is altruism, doing things for other people and not for oneself. Two Chico State University (California) professors wondered, "What motivates altruism?" To answer the question, they organized a college class at the university.

2 For the class, each student chose one altruist in the community. They spent four to five hours a week shadowing, or following, their altruist. They also went to class and read books and wrote papers on altruism.

3 Shadowing was an important part of the class. One student, Adam, followed a husband and wife. They work with many non-profit organizations in the community. Adam and the couple went shopping with elementary school children to buy holiday gifts for poor families. Adam also had dinner with the couple once a week and had many discussions with them about helping others. Two other students, Nicki and Ben, shadowed the director of a homeless shelter. The students served food to homeless people and they helped the director raise money[2] for the shelter.

4 The students learned many things. Adam said, "In school, we think too much about our careers. This class helped us remember that there are other important things in life. I also learned that I can help others as a career." Another student said, "Altruists are not necessarily special people. They are just ordinary people who do special things." The students also learned about the motivations for altruism. One altruist told a student: "I work for the community because the community helped me in the past." Another said: "I get great satisfaction[3] because I know that I am helping others. Recognition[4] for my work is not important."

5 The altruists also learned things from the students. The students' questions made them think.

A class on altruism

continued

[1] **motivates:** makes someone want to do something
[2] **raise money:** get money
[3] **satisfaction:** a good feeling
[4] **recognition:** appreciation; credit

Understanding the Text

5 | Understanding the Text

A. Write *T* for *True* and *F* for *False* according to the information in the text. Try not to look at the text. Discuss your answers with a partner.

_____ 1. Students in the class worked with altruists in the community.

_____ 2. Students did not have to read books or write papers for the class.

_____ 3. The students learned why altruists do good things.

_____ 4. The altruists did not learn very much from the students.

_____ 5. One student learned that altruism could be a career.

B. Check (✔) the characteristics of the altruists in the text. Discuss your answers with a partner.

☐ 1. They think that getting paid for their work is important.

☐ 2. They get satisfaction from helping others.

After each text, students are presented with a **two-part reading comprehension activity**. The first part checks the students' comprehension of the most basic ideas expressed in the text, whereas the second part challenges the students to recall other key ideas and information. Students are asked to complete as much as they can without looking back at the text.

4 | Understanding the Topic and the Main Idea

Answer the questions or write *T* for the *Topic*, *MI* for *Main Idea*, *G* for *Too General*, and *S* for *Too Specific*.

1. What is the topic of *Text 4*? _____

2. What is the main idea of *Text 4*?

a. _____ Students are taking a new college course.

b. _____ Students are studying other people in a new college course.

c. _____ Students are learning about altruism in a new college course.

3. Are your answers for the topic and the main idea the same as the ones you chose when you previewed the text? Explain. _____

4. What is the topic of ¶4?

a. _____ what the students learned about altruism

b. _____ what motivates altruism

c. _____ what the students learned

5. What is the main idea of ¶4?

a. _____ Altruists do not usually care about recognition for their work.

b. _____ The students learned many things about altruists and altruism.

c. _____ The students learned many things.

Understanding the Topic, Main Idea, and Supporting Details

Topic, Main Idea, and *Supporting Details* are introduced in separate chapters, allowing for **practice and mastery** before progressing to the next skill. Earlier chapters present choices in a **multiple choice format**, whereas subsequent chapters require the students to **write their own interpretations**.

7 | Understanding Subject Pronouns

Write the subject that the pronoun refers to in *Text 2*.

1. they (they can) (¶2) _____

2. They (They recommend) (¶3) _____

3. She (She makes) (¶5) _____

4. It (It gives) (¶7) _____

Practice Activities

A variety of activities allow students to practice the reading skills and vocabulary strategies, allowing for **recycling, review, and mastery**. (see *Reading Skills* and *Vocabulary Strategies* on page xi).

8 | Discussing the Issues

Answer the questions and discuss your answers with a partner.

1. Who would you nominate for a MacArthur genius grant?

2. Imagine: You won the MacArthur genius grant. What will you do with the money?

3. Think about your favorite activity. It can be something that you love to do or something that you do very well—for example, a sport or a hobby. How could you use your favorite activity to help to solve a problem? Use your imagination.

Discussing the Issues

Every text ends with a series of questions that encourage the students to **express their opinions and ideas** about the general subject discussed in the text.

Reading Skills

> ### READING SKILL Understanding Supporting Details
>
> A **supporting detail** supports a main idea. That means it proves or explains a main idea. Writers use details to develop their ideas. Supporting details can be facts, opinions, statistics, and examples.
>
> Reread ¶4 of *Text 4* on page 89.
>
> The main idea is: The students learned many things about altruists and altruism.
>
> Some of the supporting details are:
>
> 1. Adam learned that there are other things in life besides a career.
>
> 2. Another student learned that altruists are ordinary people who do special things.
>
> 3. One student learned that altruists do what they do because helping others gives them satisfaction.
>
> These details show examples of the things the students learned about altruism and altruists.

- In each chapter, students are introduced to **new reading skills and vocabulary strategies.** They are always followed by a practice activity.

- The reading skills include *Active Previewing, Skimming, Scanning, Making Inferences,* and *Understanding the Topic, Main Idea,* and *Supporting Details,* among others.

Vocabulary Strategies

> ### VOCABULARY STRATEGY Understanding Object Pronouns
>
> An **object pronoun** replaces a noun that is the object in a sentence. An object pronoun replaces a noun that comes *before* it, and it always matches the number (singular or plural) and the gender (*he, she, it*) of the noun that it replaces. The object pronouns are **me, you, him, her, it, us, you,** and **them.**
>
> Read the examples.
>
> 1. Janine Licare started a non-profit organization. She started *it* when she was nine years old.
>
> What is *it* in the second sentence? *It* is the non-profit organization in the first sentence.
>
> 2. KSTR has many volunteers. KSTR does not pay *them* for their work.
>
> What does *them* refer to in the second sentence? It refers to the volunteers in the first sentence.

6 | Understanding Object Pronouns

Write the object that the pronoun refers to in *Text 1* on pages 77–78.

1. it (with it) (¶2) _____

2. it (make it) (¶7) _____

3. them (learned from them) (¶8) _____

7 | Discussing the Issues

Answer the questions and discuss your answers with a partner.

1. Do you know of any other people or organizations that work to save the environment? If yes, tell your partner about them.

2. Do you do anything to help save the environment? For example, do you recycle paper?

3. Janine Licare says, "We have the power to change the world and make it a better place." Do you agree? Why or why not?

- Students are introduced to a variety of vocabulary strategies that can help them determine the meanings of new vocabulary **without using their dictionaries**.

- All vocabulary strategies present the vocabulary as it is used in the texts themselves, **in context**, yet the strategies themselves **can be applied universally** to reading that students do outside class.

Graphics

Students are exposed to a **variety of graphics**. Text 3 of each chapter is always a **graphical representation on the chapter's theme**.

- The graphics include *Tables, Charts, Graphs, Timelines,* and *Illustrations,* among others.

THE MOST INFLUENTIAL PEOPLE OF THE 20TH CENTURY

At the end of the 20th century, *TIME Magazine* took a poll[1]. It asked its readers: "Who were the most influential people of the century?" The chart below shows some of the results. It shows some of the top people in four categories: world leaders, business leaders, scientists and thinkers, and heroes. It shows how they ranked, the percent of votes that they received, and the total number of votes that they received ("Tally").

To *TIME Magazine*, "influential people" caused great changes in the world during the 20th century.

RANK	NAME	PERCENT	TALLY
LEADERS AND REVOLUTIONARIES[2]			
1	Winston Churchill	33.84	1,364,933
2	Franklin Roosevelt	12.25	494,096
3	Nelson Mandela	0.23	9,670
4	John Kennedy	0.21	8,634
BUILDERS AND TITANS			
1	Henry Ford	18.76	591,624
2	Bill Gates	16.49	520,151
3	Howard Hughes	11.15	351,551
4	Steve Jobs	9.58	302,256
SCIENTISTS AND THINKERS			
1	Enrico Fermi	21.25	769,453
2	Jonas Salk	21.04	762,048
3	Alan Turing	8.52	308,806
4	Albert Einstein	1.49	54,262
HEROES AND ICONS			
1	Yuri Gagarin	35.48	2,068,760
2	Mother Teresa	1.72	100,365
3	Amelia Earhart	1.56	91,290
4	Elvis Presley	0.09	5,502

[1] **took a poll:** asked a group of people a question
[2] **leader:** a person who other people follow

3 | Scanning Tables

Scan the table on page 87 to find the answers to the questions. Discuss your answers with a partner.

1. What category is Bill Gates in?
2. How
3. What
4. How
5. Who
6. What
7. Who
8. Who

> **REMEMBER**
> Scan a table with percents and use them to answer questions quickly about

---

8 | Discussing the Issues

Answer the questions and discuss your answers with a partner.

1. Who would you nominate for a MacArthur genius grant?
2. Imagine: You won the MacArthur genius grant. What will you do with the money?
3. Think about your favorite activity. It can be something that you love to do or something that you do very well—for example, a sport or a hobby. How could you use your favorite activity to help to solve a problem? Use your imagination.

Text 3 | Making a Difference

1 | Getting Started

Answer the questions and discuss your answers with a partner.

1. Make a list of ten famous people who work to solve problems in the world, your country, or your community. Think of people from the past and the present.
2. Make a list of ten famous people who cause problems in the world, your country, or your community. Think of people from the past and the present.
3. Now look at your lists. Who is the most influential (powerful or important) person on each list?

> **GRAPHICS** Understanding Tables
>
> **Tables** show statistics in different ways. In Chapters 2 and 3, you previewed tables with top-row and left-hand column headings. Some tables have subheadings—headings that show categories within a table. Subheadings are sometimes in bold type or capital letters. When you preview a table, look for subheadings.

2 | Active Previewing

Preview the table on the next page. Then answer the questions. Discuss your answers with a partner.

1. What is the title of the table? _____
2. What words are in the top row? _____
   _____
3. What do the subheadings say? _____
4. What is the topic of the table? _____

> **REMEMBER**
> Preview the table by looking at the title, especially the important words. Then look at the top-row headings and any subheadings. See page 26 for more information on *understanding and previewing tables.*

NOTE

Throughout *Well Read*, help is provided in the margin. *Remember, Note,* and *Online Tip* boxes give suggestions and page references to aid students as they work.

Putting It On Paper

A. Write a paragraph on one of these topics.

1. What is the most important problem to solve in the world today? Why is it the most important problem?

2. Can a person learn to be an altruist? Explain your answer.

Steps for your paragraph

a. State the main idea of your paragraph in the first sentence. This is your topic sentence.

b. Include in your paragraph three supporting details that explain your idea. Use facts, opinions, statistics, and/or examples.

c. Try to use words and expressions from this chapter.

B. Exchange paragraphs with a partner. Read your partner's paragraph. Answer the questions in the checklist. Give feedback to your partner.

✔ CHECKLIST
1. Is there a clear main idea?
2. Are there enough supporting details? What types of supporting details are they?
3. Do all the supporting details connect to the main idea?
4. Are there words and expressions from this chapter?
5. Write additional comments below.

C. Use y

Taking It Online | Problem Solving

A. With a partner, use the Internet to find more information about organizations or people who work to solve problems.

1. Choose a problem that interests you. Then find organizations that are working on the problem. Find out what they are doing. Find out how other people can help. For example, if you are interested in saving the rainforest, look for organizations or groups of people that are working on this.

2. Use Google (www.google.com) or another major search engine to find sites with the information you want.

3. Preview the sites as you would a magazine article.

> **ONLINE TIP**
> Combine key words:
> saving the rainforest + organizations
> weather changes + organizations
> pollution + organizations

B. Complete the table with the information you find.

Problem
The problem:
Name of Website/Name of organization:
Website address:
What kind of information does this organization have on its website?
What projects is this organization involved in?
What can people do to help solve the problem?
What can people do to help the organization?
Other facts:

C. Following up. Share your facts with your classmates. Which organizations would you like to help? Why?

Putting It On Paper

- In each chapter, students have the opportunity to write a **paragraph, letter**, or **essay** based on the chapter's theme.

- The writing activity complements the chapter texts, yet it is also **designed to stand independently** if all of the chapter texts are not covered.

- Each *Putting It On Paper* activity offers **two writing prompts**.

Taking It Online

- Every chapter culminates with a *Taking It Online* activity. This activity guides students through the steps necessary for **conducting online research**, based on the theme of the chapter.

- The online activity is **open** to the extent that students are encouraged to find their own sites, **but it is also focused** enough so that students will not be roaming through undirected data.

- *Taking It Online* finishes with a **follow-up activity** that enables students to **take their research one step further**, in pairs or groups.

The Sociology of Food

Answer the questions and discuss your answers with a partner.

1. Do you like trying different foods?

2. Look at the photos. What is happening in each of them?

3. Which photo shows a place where you would like to eat?

4. How are food and eating in the past different from food and eating today?

a

b

c

Text 1 | School Lunches

1 | Getting Started

A. Read the questions in the chart. Then fill in the chart with information from three classmates.

Questions	Name _____	Name _____	Name _____
1. When you were a child, did you… a. …eat a school lunch? b. …bring your lunch to school? c. …eat lunch at home?			
2. What did you usually eat?			
3. Where do you eat lunch now?			
4. What do you usually eat?			

B. Think about your own answers to the questions in the chart. Then discuss your answers with a partner.

 READING SKILL Previewing Articles

To **preview** an **article**, read the title. Find the important words in the title.
The important words are usually nouns, verbs, and adjectives. They often start with capital letters.

Read the following title.

<u>Schools</u> Are <u>Serving</u> <u>Healthier</u> <u>Lunches</u>

The important words in the title tell you what the text is about: schools serving healthier lunches.

2 | Active Previewing

Preview the online article on the next page. <u>Underline</u> the important words in the title. Then answer this question with a partner.

What do you think this text is about?

A. Read the text. Stop after each paragraph and tell a partner one thing that you remember about it.

School Lunches Around the World

1   Many parents worry about the food that children eat. They especially worry about the food that children get at school. Why? Health and weight are becoming a problem around the world. Many people believe that children eat too much fat, sugar, and salt, especially in school lunches.

2   This isn't a problem everywhere. In some countries, schools don't serve food to students. Some students go home for lunch, and some students bring their own lunches to school.

3   The BBC News website asked people from around the world this question: What do (or *did*) you eat at school for lunch? Here are a few answers:

- **Bruno,** 10, France: Today, we had grapefruit, grilled chicken, green beans, cheese, and pudding for dessert[1].
- **Sarah,** 8, Florida (USA): We get to choose. Today, I had pizza, salad, cake, and milk. We have a soda machine at school. I don't buy sodas. My mom doesn't let me.
- **Max,** 11, Ukraine: We start with *borscht*[2]. We usually have sausages or some other kind of meat and mashed potatoes. Today we had *syrki*[3] for dessert.
- **Wei,** 25, Massachusetts (USA): In China, where I grew up, students went home for lunch. Parents also came home for lunch, so we usually ate a good home-cooked[4] meal.
- **Ping,** 23, Taiwan: In Taiwan, children under 12 have lunch in school. Usually there is rice, two kinds of vegetables, one kind of meat, and a bowl of soup. You can eat like you eat at home.
- **Laura,** 32, Puerto Rico: My daughter usually has rice and beans, salad, and chicken for lunch at school. It comes with milk, but she never drinks it. The government tried to include fast food[5] in school lunches, but the parents didn't allow it.

---

[1] **dessert:** a (usually) sweet food; it comes after the main meal
[2] **borscht:** a kind of soup
[3] **syrki:** [*seer kee*] chocolate-covered cream cheese
[4] **home-cooked:** cooked at home
[5] **fast food:** food that is prepared and served quickly; usually has a lot of calories but isn't healthy

B. Read the text again without stopping. Tell your partner two new pieces of information that you remember.

C. Work as a class or in large groups. Try to name as many things as you can about the text.

4 | Understanding the Text

A. Answer this question without looking at the text. Discuss your answers with a partner.

What is the text about?

    a. unhealthy school lunches

    b. types of school lunches in different countries

    c. children's health and weight problems

B. Match each statement with one or more of the people. Discuss your answers with a partner.

Statement	People
_a, b, c_ 1. has dessert with lunch	a. Bruno
_____ 2. drinks milk with lunch	b. Sarah
_____ 3. eats/ate lunch at home	c. Max
_____ 4. has salad with lunch	d. Wei
_____ 5. has fruit with lunch	e. Ping
_____ 6. has soup with lunch	f. Laura's daughter

5 | Discussing the Issues

Answer the questions and discuss your answers with a partner.

1. Which children in the text have healthy lunches? Why are the lunches healthy?

2. Which lunch would you like to eat? Why?

3. Should children have sodas, fast food, or desserts at school? Why or why not?

Text 2 | Restaurant Fare

1 | Getting Started

A. Answer the questions and discuss your answers with a partner.

1. What foods did your grandparents eat? Can you still find these foods today? Are they different from the foods that you eat?

2. Think about three restaurants: one from the 1900s, one from the 1950s, and one today. How might they be different from each other?

B. Check (✔) the types of food you have tried or want to try. Add more types of food. Discuss your answers with a partner.

Have you tried these types of food?	Tried	Want to try
1. French (from France)	☐	☐
2. Japanese (from Japan)	☐	☐
3. Moroccan (from Morocco)	☐	☐
4. Mexican (from Mexico)	☐	☐
5. Indian (from India)	☐	☐
6.	☐	☐
7.	☐	☐

VOCABULARY STRATEGY Skipping Words

Skipping words is a useful reading strategy. When you read, you do not need to know every word. Decide: Is the word important? If not, skip it. You can often understand the meaning of a sentence without knowing every word in it.

Read this sentence:

We usually have *sausages* or some other kind of meat and mashed potatoes.

Do you know what *sausages* are? If not, does it matter? No. You can tell that it is something to eat, probably meat.

2 | Skipping Words

Read the following sentences from *Text 2*. Underline the words that you do not know. Can you still understand the sentence? Check (✔) *Yes* or *No*.

1. The meal included soup, fish, an entree, vegetables, dessert, and a drink.

   ☐ a. Yes   ☐ b. No

2. Today, it is very difficult to find *fricadellen* (a kind of Dutch meatball) in the U.S.

   ☐ a. Yes   ☐ b. No

3. Very few people drink buttermilk (the liquid that is left after cream becomes butter).

   ☐ a. Yes   ☐ b. No

4. Some people had a French-style dessert called crepes suzette.

   ☐ a. Yes   ☐ b. No

5. Lobster Thermador and crepes suzette are old-fashioned dishes, but you might still find them on some menus.

   ☐ a. Yes   ☐ b. No

3 | Active Previewing

Preview the magazine article below. <u>Underline</u> the important words in the title. Then answer this question with a partner.

What do you think this text is about?

4 | Reading and Recalling

A. Read the text. Stop after each paragraph and tell a partner one thing that you remember about it.

Restaurants, Then and Now

1   Restaurants 100 years ago were very different from restaurants today. Let's take a look at three examples from Southern California. One is from the 1900s, one is from the 1950s, and one is from the 2000s.

2 **1900s: The Royal Restaurant, Los Angeles, CA**

A hundred years ago in the United States, people ate a lot of food. They liked foods from home, and home was often "the Old Country[1]" or a farm. People found food like this at the Royal Restaurant. The Royal Restaurant served a complete lunch. The meal included soup, fish, an entree[2], vegetables, dessert, and a drink. At the Royal Restaurant, people ate *fricadellen* and *muskmelon*. They drank buttermilk. Today, it is very difficult to find *fricadellen* (a kind of Dutch meatball) on an American menu. *Muskmelon* (a fruit) is now called cantaloupe. And today, very few people drink buttermilk (the liquid that is left after cream becomes butter).

3 **1950s: The Mocambo, Hollywood, CA**

In the 1950s, more people in the U.S. had money to eat well. They were interested in foreign food. They were especially interested in French food. The Mocambo in Hollywood was a typical fancy restaurant in the 1950s. Movie stars such as Humphrey Bogart, Clark Gable, and Judy Garland ate at the Mocambo. The Mocambo served the stars elegant[3] dishes. For dinner, people often started with a half of a grapefruit. They had Lobster Thermador Prince de Monaco, lobster in a sauce. (The name of this dish came from a real prince who married a movie star.) Some people had a French-style dessert called crepes suzette. These are thin pancakes with an orange sauce. Today, Americans mostly eat grapefruit for breakfast, not dinner. Lobster Thermador and crepes suzette are old-fashioned dishes, but you might still find them on some menus.

4 **2000s: *five sixty one*, Pasadena, CA**

In the 2000s, Americans are trying to eat less. They are trying to eat healthy food. And they are interested in foods from all over the world. The *five sixty one* restaurant is an example of a modern restaurant. It serves healthy dishes in ethnic[4] styles. For example, at *five sixty one*, you can start with Tuna Tataki. This is a Japanese-style salad with seaweed. Next, you can have Vegetable Tagine Casablanca. This is a Moroccan-style vegetarian[5] dish. A meal at *five sixty one* costs twice as much as a meal at the Mocambo in the 1950s, and it costs about 100 times more than a meal at the Royal Restaurant in the 1900s!

Muskmelon (a fruit) is now called cantaloupe.

---

[1] **the Old Country:** a phrase people sometimes use to talk about the country where they were born
[2] **entree:** main dish
[3] **elegant:** very nice; expensive; high quality
[4] **ethnic:** from a particular culture
[5] **vegetarian:** without meat

B. Read the text again without stopping. Tell your partner two new pieces of information that you remember.

C. Work as a class or in large groups. Try to name as many things as you can about the text.

5 | Understanding the Text

A. Answer as many questions as you can without looking at the text. Discuss your answers with a partner.

1. What is the text about?

   a. some differences between restaurants today and restaurants in the past

   b. foods that movie stars in the 1950s ate

   c. popular ethnic dishes at modern restaurants

2. What is one difference between restaurants today and restaurants in the past?

   a. Today, restaurants serve food from different countries.

   b. Today, restaurants name dishes after movie stars.

   c. Today, restaurant meals cost more.

B. Check (✔) the correct answers according to the text. Discuss your answers with a partner.

Which restaurant...	The Royal	The Mocambo	*five sixty one*
1. ... serves/served food from different countries or cultures?	✔	✔	✔
2. ... serves/served dishes for people who do not eat meat?	☐	☐	☐
3. ... serves/served food to movie stars?	☐	☐	☐
4. ... serves/served food that people ate at home or on a farm?	☐	☐	☐
5. ... serves/served fruit?	☐	☐	☐

6 | Discussing the Issues

Answer the questions and discuss your answers with a partner.

1. At which restaurant would you like to eat: the Royal, the Mocambo, or *five sixty one*? Why?

2. Did you ever eat any of the dishes you read about in the text? If yes, which ones? Did you like them?

3. Think about a culture you know. In that culture, do people have the same ways of eating that they had in the past? Explain.

Text 3 | Food Inventions

1 | Getting Started

Answer the questions and discuss your answers with a partner. If you are not sure, guess.

1. When did people first use dishwashers? Microwaves?

2. When did soft drinks first come in cans?

3. Who were the first people to freeze food?

 GRAPHICS Understanding Timelines

Timelines show times in history and events (things that happened). They show the times and the events in a horizontal line ⟷ or in a vertical line ↕. To **preview** a timeline, look at the title, especially the important words.

Then look at the dates in the line, especially the first and last dates. Also, look for any **boldfaced** words or expressions.

2 | Active Previewing

Preview the timeline and then answer the questions. Discuss your answers with a partner.

1. What is the title of the timeline? Underline the important words. _____

2. What is the first date in the timeline? _____

3. What is the last date in the timeline? _____

4. What are some of the boldfaced words and expressions? List five of them. _____

5. What is the timeline about?

    a. the invention of the dishwasher

    b. food inventions in the last 100 years

    c. recent food inventions

 READING SKILL Scanning

Scanning is moving your eyes quickly over a page. You scan to find the information you are looking for, such as the name of a person or a company. When you scan, you do not read every word. If you are looking for names of people, look only for words that begin with capital letters.

Scan the following sentence to answer this question: Who invented the dishwasher? Remember: Do not read every word.

Josephine Cochran invented the first dishwashing machine.

The answer is *Josephine Cochran*.

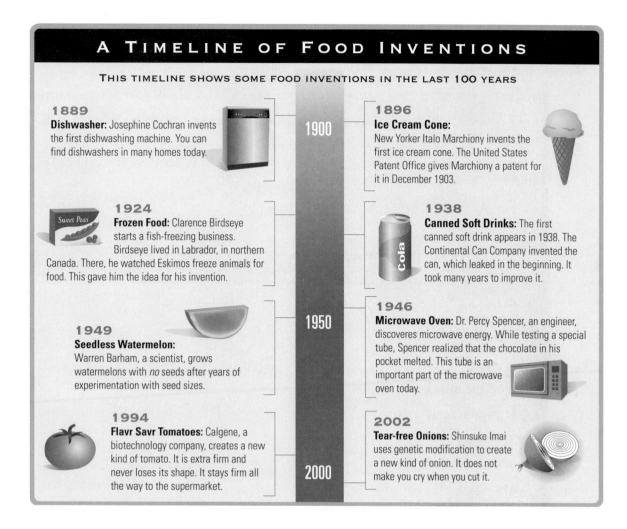

A Timeline of Food Inventions

THIS TIMELINE SHOWS SOME FOOD INVENTIONS IN THE LAST 100 YEARS

1889
Dishwasher: Josephine Cochran invents the first dishwashing machine. You can find dishwashers in many homes today.

1896
Ice Cream Cone: New Yorker Italo Marchiony invents the first ice cream cone. The United States Patent Office gives Marchiony a patent for it in December 1903.

1924
Frozen Food: Clarence Birdseye starts a fish-freezing business. Birdseye lived in Labrador, in northern Canada. There, he watched Eskimos freeze animals for food. This gave him the idea for his invention.

1938
Canned Soft Drinks: The first canned soft drink appears in 1938. The Continental Can Company invented the can, which leaked in the beginning. It took many years to improve it.

1949
Seedless Watermelon: Warren Barham, a scientist, grows watermelons with *no* seeds after years of experimentation with seed sizes.

1946
Microwave Oven: Dr. Percy Spencer, an engineer, discoveres microwave energy. While testing a special tube, Spencer realized that the chocolate in his pocket melted. This tube is an important part of the microwave oven today.

1994
Flavr Savr Tomatoes: Calgene, a biotechnology company, creates a new kind of tomato. It is extra firm and never loses its shape. It stays firm all the way to the supermarket.

2002
Tear-free Onions: Shinsuke Imai uses genetic modification to create a new kind of onion. It does not make you cry when you cut it.

1900 — 1950 — 2000

3 | Scanning

Scan the timeline to answer the questions. Discuss your answers with a partner.

1. Who invented the ice cream cone? _____

2. Who invented frozen food? _____

3. Who invented the seedless watermelon? _____

4. Which company created a new kind of tomato? _____

5. Who invented a tear-free onion? _____

4 | Understanding the Graphics

Answer as many questions as you can. Discuss your answers with a partner.

1. Which inventions are things to eat or drink? _____

2. Which inventions are machines? _____

3. Which invention was an accident? _____

4. Which invention did not work at first? _____

5. Which invention came from someone else's idea? _____

5 | Discussing the Issues

Answer the questions and discuss your answers with a partner.

1. Go back to the questions from *Getting Started* on page 8. Were any of your answers correct?

2. Give your opinion: Which invention in the timeline is the most important? Why? Which invention is the least important? Why?

3. What are some other important food inventions? What might be some food inventions in the future?

Text 4 | The History of the Restaurant

1 | Getting Started

A. Work with a partner. Match the type of restaurant with the photo. Then answer the questions on the next page.

_____ **1.** a restaurant

_____ **2.** a diner

_____ **3.** a tavern

_____ **4.** a cafe

1. What do people eat or drink at each type of restaurant? What else might people do at each place?

2. How are the places similar to or different from each other?

B. Take the quiz. Guess *T* for *True* or *F* for *False*. Discuss your answers with a partner.

_____ 1. There were restaurants in the ancient world.

_____ 2. The word *restaurant* comes from a French word.

_____ 3. In France, the first restaurants served only soup.

_____ 4. Before the 18th century, restaurants did not have menus.

_____ 5. Before the 18th century, people did not know the cost of restaurant food before they ate it.

2 | Skipping Words

Read the following sentences from *Text 4*. Underline the words that you do not know. Can you still understand the sentence? Check (✔) *Yes* or *No*.

1. Taverns served simple meals and drinks to travelers.

   ☐ a. Yes   ☐ b. No

2. Also for the first time, customers knew how much the food cost before they ate it.

   ☐ a. Yes   ☐ b. No

3. This soup was restorative; this means, it made people feel better when they were tired or sick.

   ☐ a. Yes   ☐ b. No

4. Before the revolution, many rich people had chefs in their homes.

   ☐ a. Yes   ☐ b. No

5. There are even restaurants that show movies, restaurants where people eat in the dark, and underwater restaurants.

   ☐ a. Yes   ☐ b. No

3 | Active Previewing

Preview the academic text on the next page. Underline the important words in the title. Then answer the following question with a partner.

What do you think this text is about?

> **REMEMBER**
> Find the important words in the title.
> For more information on *previewing articles*, see page 2.

4 | Reading and Recalling

A. Read the text. Stop after each paragraph and tell a partner one thing that you remember about it.

The History of the Restaurant

1   According to the dictionary, a restaurant is an eating place. Therefore, according to this definition, the restaurant is as old as civilization[1]. For example, there is evidence of[2] eating places in ancient Roman ruins.

2   Most ancient eating places were taverns. Taverns served simple meals and drinks to travelers. By the middle of the 17th century, a new kind of eating place appeared in many parts of Europe. These were cafes. At first, they served only coffee; later, they served food. Cafes became popular meeting places for writers and their friends.

3   The restaurant appeared at the end of the 18th century, in Paris. It was very different from the tavern or the cafe. It gave customers a choice. Restaurants had menus. For the first time, customers decided what to eat, when to eat, and how much to eat. Also for the first time, customers knew how much the food cost before they ate it. The menu at a typical Parisian restaurant in the 18th century might have 12 different kinds of soup, 65 meat dishes, and 50 desserts.

4   Before the restaurant was born, there were different kinds of cooks in France. For example, there were roasters, bakers, and dessert makers. A roaster could not bake anything and a baker could not make a dessert. This was the law. Also at this time, the word *restaurant* had a special meaning. It was a French word for a kind of soup. This soup was restorative; this means, it made people feel better when they were tired or sick. Eating places served the restorative soup to customers.

5   In 1765, a man named Boulanger owned one of these soup shops. One day, he broke the law[3]. He cooked some meat and put a sauce on it. This made the sauce makers angry. They went to court. Boulanger won, and the modern restaurant was born. By 1786, a restaurant was a place to cook and serve all types of foods and drinks: soups, meats, salads, desserts, and wines.

6   An important time for the restaurant was the French Revolution, around 1792. Before the revolution, many rich people had chefs in their homes. The French Revolution ended the monarchy[4] and the aristocracy[5]. After the revolution, many chefs did not have jobs, so they started restaurants. As a result, restaurants became an important kind of business in France. Now, eating well was for everyone, not just rich people.

7   By the 19th century, there were many restaurants in Paris and in many big cities around the world. Restaurants became more than just places to eat; they became places to meet people and to try new things.

8   Today, the word *restaurant* can mean many things—a diner, a cafeteria, or a place to eat fast food. There are even restaurants that show movies, restaurants where people eat in the dark, and underwater restaurants. Who knows what will happen in the restaurant world of the future?

---

[1] **as old as civilization:** since the time of the first human cultures
[2] **evidence of:** proof of
[3] **broke the law:** did something illegal
[4] **monarchy:** ruling by kings and queens
[5] **aristocracy:** upper classes

B. Read the text again without stopping. Tell your partner two new pieces of information that you remember.

C. Work as a class or in large groups. Try to say as many things as you can about the text.

5 | Understanding the Text

A. Complete as many sentences as you can without looking at the text. Discuss your answers with a partner.

1. The modern restaurant

   a. was born in ancient Rome.

   b. was born in France.

   c. was born in the 19th century.

2. Restaurants were different from taverns and cafes because

   a. they served food.

   b. they were only for travelers.

   c. people had choices.

3. At first, the word *restaurant* meant

   a. a place to eat many kinds of food.

   b. a kind of soup.

   c. a place to eat meat with sauce.

4. Boulanger changed the idea of the restaurant by

   a. starting a revolution.

   b. opening a soup shop.

   c. breaking the law.

5. After the French Revolution,

   a. many chefs needed work.

   b. many rich people needed work.

   c. Boulanger needed work.

6. Now, the word *restaurant* means

   a. a diner.

   b. a cafeteria.

   c. a place to eat fast food.

   d. all of the above.

B. Complete the timeline according to the text. Put the events next to the correct time periods in the chart. Discuss your answers with a partner.

a. ~~Taverns serve food to travelers.~~

b. French-style restaurants appear around the world.

c. The restaurant becomes a place to serve all kinds of food.

d. Cafes appear in Europe.

e. The French Revolution happens.

f. Boulanger serves meat with a sauce at his soup shop.

Time period	Event
1. Ancient times	a. Taverns serve food to travelers.
2. Mid-17th century	
3. 1765	
4. 1786	
5. 1792	
6. 19th century	

6 | Discussing the Issues

Answer the questions and discuss your answers with a partner.

1. Go back to part *B* in *Getting Started* on page 11. Were any of your answers correct? (Note: All the answers are true.)

2. Did any information in the text surprise you? If yes, what information?

3. Invent a new kind of restaurant: What does it look like? What kind of food does it serve? What else can people do at the restaurant? How is it different from any other restaurant?

Putting It On Paper

A. Write a paragraph on one of these topics.

1. Describe your favorite restaurant. Explain why you like it.

2. What is the most useful food invention? Explain why it is the most useful.

Steps for your paragraph

    a. State the main idea of your paragraph in the first sentence. This is your topic sentence.

    b. Include in your paragraph three details that explain your idea.

B. Exchange paragraphs with a partner. Read your partner's paragraph. Answer the questions in the checklist. Then give feedback to your partner.

✔ CHECKLIST
1. Is there a clear main idea?
2. Are there enough details?
3. Do all the details connect to the main idea?
4. Write additional comments below.

_____

_____

_____

_____

_____

_____

_____

_____

_____

C. After listening to your partner's feedback, do you want to revise, or make changes, to your work?

A. With a partner, use the Internet to find more information about restaurants.

1. Choose a type of restaurant—for example, a fast-food restaurant, a diner, or a cafe. Find out about the history of this type of restaurant.

2. Use Google (www.google.com) or another major search engine to find sites with the information you want.

3. Preview the sites the same way you would preview a magazine article.

> **ONLINE TIP**
>
> Combine key words:
> history + fast food
>   restaurant
> history + diner
> history + cafe
> You do not need "little" words like *of* and *the*.

B. Complete the table with the information you find.

Restaurant
Type of restaurant:
Name of Website:
Website address:
Where did this type of restaurant first appear?
When did this type of restaurant first appear?
What other events were happening at this time?
Who invented it? Who had the first restaurant of this type?
Other facts:

C. Following up. Share your facts with your classmates. Which type of restaurant do you like to go to the most? Why?

Technology in Movies

Answer the questions and discuss your answers with a partner.

1. Do you like movies that are not like real life?

2. Look at the photos. What is happening in each of them?

3. How did the filmmakers create scenes like the ones in photos *b* and *c*?

4. What are some other movies with special effects?

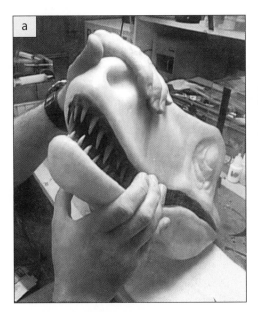

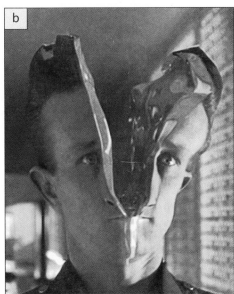

Text 1 | A Movie Classic

1 | Getting Started

A. Look at the photos. Then answer the questions below in small groups.

1. Match the movie title with the photo.

_____ *King Kong,* 1933

_____ *King Kong,* 2005

2. What is happening in the photos?

3. Did you see these movies? If yes, tell your classmates about them.

B. Answer the questions and then discuss your answers with a partner.

1. How are these movies the same?

2. How are these movies different?

3. Do you think movie *a* and movie *b* cost the same amount of money to make? Why or why not?

4. Do you think movie *a* and movie *b* took the same amount of time to make? Why or why not?

VOCABULARY STRATEGY Skipping Words

When you read, you do not need to know every word. You can often **skip words** you do not know and still understand the meaning of a sentence.

However, if you cannot understand the sentence, follow these steps:

1. Try to figure out the part of speech of the skipped words or phrases (noun, adjective, verb, adverb).

2. Ask yourself: "What *do* I understand?"

3. Keep reading.

Read this sentence:

Many movies are xxxxxx in film history because of their special effects.

What word is missing? Can you guess what part of speech it is? It comes after a form of the verb *be*, so it is probably a noun or an adjective. Because there is no article (*a, an, the*), the missing word is probably an adjective. What do you understand about the sentence? You can understand this: Many movies are *famous* or *important* in film history because of their special effects. At this point, you have enough information to keep reading.

2 | Skipping Words

A. Read the following sentences from *Text 1*. Check (✔) the part of speech of the missing word.

1. The xxxxxxxxxx made many of the FX scenes in the original *King Kong* in two days.

   ☐ a. noun   ☐ b. adjective

2. Today, similar scenes in modern films might take two weeks to xxxxxx.

   ☐ a. noun   ☐ b. verb

3. In *King Kong*, a man finds a xxxxxxxx gorilla, King Kong, in Africa.

   ☐ a. noun   ☐ b. adjective

4. FX scenes show Kong xxxxx xxxx dinosaurs, a giant snake, and a flying reptile.

   ☐ a. noun   ☐ b. verb

5. In many scenes, King Kong was only an 18-inch xxxxx, but he looked 50 feet tall.

   ☐ a. noun   ☐ b. adjective

B. Discuss your answers with a partner. Give reasons for your guesses.

3 | Active Previewing

Preview the online article on the next page. <u>Underline</u> the important words in the title. Then answer the question with a partner.

What do you think this text is about?

4 | Reading and Recalling

A. Read the text. Stop after each paragraph and tell a partner one thing that you remember about it.

King Kong: A Movie Classic[1]

REMEMBER

Skip words that you do not understand. See page 19 for more information on *skipping words*.

1   You can see almost anything in movies today: People fly in the air. Monsters appear from nowhere. Animals talk. Movies can make the impossible seem possible. How? Special effects. Many movies are famous in film history because of their special effects. *King Kong* (1933) is one of these. *King Kong* was one of the first movies with special effects. *King Kong* led to many of the special effects (FX) techniques[2] in modern movies such as *Jurassic Park* and *Alien*.

2   Most critics agree: the dialog[3] and acting in *King Kong* weren't very good. However, there is some kind of special effect in almost every scene. For 1933, this was very unusual. It looked like an expensive movie, but it cost only $600,000 to make. (To compare, the 2005 *King Kong* by Peter Jackson cost over $200 million to make.) The filmmakers made many of the FX scenes in the original *King Kong* in two days. Today, similar scenes in modern films might take two weeks to create.

3   In *King Kong*, a man finds a gigantic gorilla, King Kong, in Africa. He takes the gorilla to New York City. King Kong escapes and terrorizes[4] the city. FX scenes show Kong fight with dinosaurs, a giant snake, and a flying reptile. Later in the movie, the giant gorilla climbs to the top of the Empire State Building and holds a tiny woman. In many scenes, King Kong was only an 18-inch model, but he looked 50 feet tall. The movie actually frightened many audience members.

4   *King Kong* isn't a perfect movie. But the story and FX scenes still affect[5] audiences. This is why it will always be a great movie classic.

---

[1] **a movie classic:** a movie that is popular for a long time
[2] **techniques:** ways of doing things
[3] **dialog:** the speaking parts in a movie
[4] **terrorizes:** frightens
[5] **affect:** influence; have an effect on

B. Read the text again without stopping. Tell your partner two new pieces of information that you remember.

C. Work as a class or in large groups. Try to say as many things as you can about the text.

5 | Understanding the Text

Answer as many questions as you can without looking at the text. Discuss your answers with a partner.

1. What is the text about?

   a. why the 1933 movie *King Kong* is famous

   b. the differences between the 1933 *King Kong* and the 2005 *King Kong*

   c. the special effects in *King Kong*

2. Why was the 1933 *King Kong* unusual?

   a. because it had so many special effects

   b. because it took a short time to make the movie

   c. because the movie was inexpensive to make

3. How much did the 2005 *King Kong* cost to make?

   a. $200

   b. $200,000

   c. $200 million

4. In one scene in the 1933 *King Kong*, what did the filmmakers use?

   a. an 18-inch model of a gorilla

   b. a 50-foot model of a gorilla

   c. a real gorilla

5. What did many audience members think about the FX in 1933 *King Kong*?

   a. They didn't like the FX.

   b. They thought that the FX were frightening.

   c. They thought that the FX were not very believable.

6. Why will the 1933 *King Kong* always be a movie classic?

   a. because of the actors and the acting

   b. because of the dialog

   c. because of the story and the FX

6 | Discussing the Issues

Answer the questions and discuss your answers with a partner.

1. If you saw the 1933 *King Kong*, what did you think about it? If you did not see it, would you like to? Why or why not?

2. Do you like movies with lots of FX? Why or why not?

3. Are FX becoming more realistic? Give some examples to support your answer.

Text 2 | A Special Effects Genius

1 | Getting Started

Look at the photos. Discuss your answers with a partner.

1. Did you see any of these movies? If yes, which ones? If no, which ones would you like to see?

2. What type of person do you think made these movies?

3. Would you like to make movies? Why or why not?

4. How do you thin k the filmmaker created each of these scenes?

A scene from *Beast from 20,000 Fathoms*

A scene from *The Voyage of Sinbad*

A scene from *Clash of the Titans*

Ray Harryhausen, FX specialist, working on *Jason and the Argonauts*

2 | Skipping Words

A. Read the following sentences from *Text 2*. Guess the part of speech of the missing word. Check (✔) your answer.

1. Just about everyone in the xxxxx of special effects respects Ray Harryhausen.

☐ a. noun ☐ b. adjective

2. He saw *The Lost World* in 1925 and the special effects xxxxxxxxx him.

☐ a. noun ☐ b. verb

3. Ackerman introduced Ray to science fiction, and the two xxxxxx friends for life.

☐ a. noun ☐ b. verb

4. Ray used fur from one of his mother's xxxxx to make the model.

☐ a. noun ☐ b. adjective

5. In the 1950s, movie audiences xxxxx science fiction.

☐ a. noun ☐ b. verb

B. Discuss your answers with a partner. Give reasons for your guesses.

3 | Active Previewing

Preview the magazine article on the next page. <u>Underline</u> the important words in the title. Then answer the following question with a partner.

What do you think this text is about?

4 | Reading and Recalling

A. Read the text. Stop after each paragraph and tell a partner one thing that you remember about it.

Ray Harryhausen, Special Effects Genius[1]

1   Just about everyone in the field of special effects respects Ray Harryhausen. Ray Harryhausen is famous for his stop-motion FX technique—turning the camera off, changing a scene, and turning the camera on again.

2 Growing Up

   Ray was born in Los Angeles in 1920. He saw *The Lost World* in 1925 and the special effects impressed him. In 1933, Ray saw *King Kong.* In the lobby[2], there was a collection of stills, pictures from the film. The pictures inspired Ray. He asked the theater manager if he could borrow them. The theater manager said no because he didn't own the stills, but he gave Ray the name of the person who did—Forrest Ackerman. Ackerman loaned Ray the pictures. Ackerman introduced Ray to science fiction, and the two became friends for life.

3   In his teens, Ray learned a lot about special effects by himself. He did experiments with special effects in his backyard. He made models and studied photography. At the age of 19, he had an idea for a film about a creature from Jupiter. He never made the film, but he made all the sketches, or drawings, for the film and created a model of the creature.

4 The First Big Project

   His first big project was called *Evolution.* He planned to make a history of the beginning of the world. His favorite part was making models of dinosaurs, ancient extinct[3] reptiles. He also made a wooly mammoth—an extinct type of elephant—covered with fur. Ray used fur from one of his mother's coats to make the model. He never completed this project, but he used the models for it. Later, he went to get jobs, and he took the models with him to show his work.

> Ray used fur from one of his mother's coats to make the model.

5 Career Success

   In the 1950s, movie audiences loved science fiction. In 1953, Ray made a movie called *Beast from 20,000 Fathoms.* In the movie, a giant octopus destroys[4] the Golden Gate Bridge. To save money, he made the octopus with only six tentacles, or arms. Moviegoers didn't notice.

6   Ray went on to make many important movies. He made *The Voyage of Sinbad, Jason and the Argonauts,* and, his last movie, *Clash of the Titans.* These are all movies about great legends[5]. In the world of special effects, Ray is a legend, too.

---

[1] **genius:** a very smart person
[2] **lobby:** the entrance to a movie theater (or a hotel)
[3] **extinct:** not living any more
[4] **destroys:** ruins; breaks up
[5] **legend:** a story or person that people talk about for a long time

B. Read the text again without stopping. Tell your partner two new pieces of information that you remember.

C. Work as a class or in large groups. Try to say as many things as you can about the text.

5 | Understanding the Text

A. Answer the questions without looking at the text. Discuss your answers with a partner.

1. What is the text about?

    a. how to make special effects

    b. how to be a special effects genius

    c. the life of a special effects genius

2. What is the most important idea in the text?

    a. Harryhausen's friendship with Forrest Ackerman made him famous in the world of special effects.

    b. Harryhausen's life experiences and work made him famous in the world of special effects.

    c. Harryhausen's study of photography made him famous in the world of special effects.

B. Answer as many questions as you can without looking at the text. Discuss your answers with a partner.

1. What special effect technique made Roy Harryhausen famous? _____

    _____

2. Which movie did he see when he was 5 years old? _____

3. What was his first big project? Did he complete it? _____

4. How did Ray Harryhausen save money with *Beast from 20,000 Fathoms*? _____

    _____

5. What are three of his most important movies? _____

    _____

 VOCABULARY STRATEGY Understanding Vocabulary in Context—Synonyms

Sometimes you can understand a new word or expression from a **synonym**—a word or expression that has the same or a similar meaning.

Read these sentences:

In 1933, Ray saw *King Kong*. In the lobby, there was a collection of *stills*, pictures from the film.

If you do not know the word *stills*, you can guess because *pictures from the film* means the same thing.

6 | Understanding Vocabulary in Context—Synonyms

A. Read the following sentences from *Text 2*. Check (✔) the part of speech of the underlined words and expressions.

1. Ray Harryhausen is famous for his <u>stop-motion FX technique</u>—turning the camera off, changing a scene, and turning the camera on again.

   ☐ a. noun ☐ b. verb ☐ c. adjective

   _____

2. He never made the film, but he made all the <u>sketches</u>, or drawings, for the film and created a model of the creature.

   ☐ a. noun ☐ b. verb ☐ c. adjective

   _____

3. He also made <u>a wooly mammoth</u>—an extinct type of elephant—covered with fur.

   ☐ a. noun ☐ b. verb ☐ c. adjective

   _____

4. To save money, he made the octopus with only six <u>tentacles</u>, or arms.

   ☐ a. noun ☐ b. verb ☐ c. adjective

   _____

B. Find the synonyms for the underlined words and write them on the lines.

7 | Discussing the Issues

Answer the questions and discuss your answers with a partner.

1. What kind of person would be good at making special effects movies?

2. Do you think it is important to start young to have a career in special effects? Why or why not?

3. Imagine: You and your partner are making a movie with special effects. What is the movie about? What special effects do you want? Who will star in your movie?

Text 3 | Special Effects Statistics

1 | Getting Started

Answer the questions and discuss your answers with a partner.

1. How often do you go to the movies?

2. How much does a movie ticket usually cost?

3. Why does the cost of movie tickets keep going up?

 GRAPHICS Understanding and Previewing Tables

Tables usually show statistics—information in numbers. They show information in rows and columns. The top row and left-hand column tell you the kinds of information that the numbers show. To **preview** a table, look at the title, especially the important words. Then look at the words in the top row and in the left-hand column and any **boldfaced** or *italicized* information.

2 | Active Previewing

Preview the table on the next page and then answer the questions. Discuss your answers with a partner.

1. What is the title of the table? Underline the important words in it.

2. What words are in the top row of the table? _____

_____

3. What kind of information is in the left-hand column? Give three examples.

_____

4. What is the table about?

   a. the cost of making some movies with special effects and the money that they made

   b. the cost of making *Jurassic Park* and the money that it made

   c. the cost of making special effects and the money that they can make

THE COST OF SPECIAL EFFECTS

The cost of making movies with special effects is higher every year. Sometimes, the cost of making a movie with special effects is higher than the amount of money that the movie makes. Who pays for all of these special effects? You do! As the cost of making movies goes up, movie ticket prices go up, too. Here are some statistics on movies with special effects:

Title	Year Released	Cost of Making the Movie	Total Amount Earned[1]
Jurassic Park	1993	$63 m[2]	$915 m
Titanic	1997	$200 m	$1.8 b[3]
The Matrix	1999	$63 m	$460 m
Mission to Mars	2000	$90 m	$61 m
The Mummy Returns	2001	$100 m	$419 m
AI: Artificial Intelligence	2001	$100 m	$79 m
The Lord of the Rings: Return of the King	2003	$94 m	$1.1 b
King Kong	2005	$207 m	$549 m
Star Wars Episode 3: Revenge of the Sith	2005	$113 m	$380 m
Harry Potter and the Goblet of Fire	2005	$150 m	$892 m

Note: Amounts are rounded up[4]. Amounts are in U.S. dollars.

[1] **earned:** made
[2] **m:** million
[3] **b:** billion
[4] **rounded up:** shown in the next highest whole number

READING SKILL Scanning Tables

Scanning is looking for information quickly before or after you read a text. You can scan for numbers, symbols, bolded items, names, key words, or answers to questions.

To scan a table:

1. Decide: What do I want to find? For example, do I want to find a date, the name of a company, or the cost of making *Titanic*?

2. Predict: What signal will I be looking for? For example, capital letters, numbers, or symbols.

3. Move your eyes quickly across the page, with the help of your finger or a pencil, if you want. Look only for the item that you want to find.

Read this question.

In what year was *Jurassic Park* released?

To find the answer, scan the top row for *Year*. Scan the left-hand column for the movie title *Jurassic Park*. In this way, you find the answer: *1993*.

3 | Scanning Tables

Scan the table for the answers to the questions. Discuss your answers with a partner.

1. Which movie cost the most to make? How much did this movie earn? _____

2. Which movie earned the highest amount of money? How much did it cost to make this movie? _____

3. Which movie earned the second-highest amount of money? How much did it cost to make this movie? _____

4. Which two movies cost the same amount of money to make? Which one earned more?

   _____

5. Which two movies earned less than the cost to make them? _____

4 | Discussing the Issues

Answer the questions and discuss your answers with a partner.

1. Do special effects always make a movie better? Why or why not?

2. Did you see any of the movies in the table? If yes, give your opinion of the special effects. Were they an important part of the movie?

3. Why might a movie with a lot of special effects make very little money?

Text 4 | Secrets from FX Experts

1 | Getting Started

A. Work with a partner. Match the movie titles with the posters. Then answer the question below.

_____ **1.** *The Wizard of Oz*   _____ **2.** *Jurassic Park*   _____ **3.** *The Wolf Man*

What do you know about these movies? Discuss them with your partner.

B. Answer the questions and discuss your answers with a partner.

1. In *The Wolf Man*, an actor becomes an animal. How do you think the filmmaker made this happen?

2. In *The Wizard of Oz*, a witch disappears. How do you think the filmmaker made this happen?

3. In *Jurassic Park*, the dinosaurs look real. How did the filmmakers do that?

2 | Understanding Vocabulary in Context—Synonyms

A. Read the following sentences from *Text 4*. Check (✔) the part of speech for the underlined words.

1. Now he's a <u>werewolf</u>, a creature that is half-man, half-wolf.

   ☐ a. noun   ☐ b. verb   ☐ c. adjective

   _____

2. First, with the camera off, the makeup artists <u>applied</u> a little hair and put on slightly longer teeth.

   ☐ a. noun   ☐ b. verb   ☐ c. adjective

   _____

3. In one scene, a dinosaur—a <u>Tyrannosaurus rex</u>—attacks a man.

   ☐ a. noun   ☐ b. verb   ☐ c. adjective

   _____

4. FX specialists studied the work of <u>paleontologists</u>, people who study ancient animals.

   ☐ a. noun   ☐ b. verb   ☐ c. adjective

   _____

5. They made the models move with <u>hydraulic systems</u>—systems that use the force of water to make machines move.

   ☐ a. noun   ☐ b. verb   ☐ c. adjective

   _____

B. Find the synonyms for the underlined words and write them on the lines.

READING SKILL Previewing Headings

Headings are titles for sections of a text. They separate the different sections and tell the reader the most important ideas in each section. If you read the headings before you read the whole text, you can get a good idea of what the text is about.

Read these headings from "Ray Harryhausen: Special Effects Genius."

Growing Up • The First Big Project • Career Success

They tell you that the passage is about Harryhausen's childhood, his early work, and his success in the field of FX.

Note: Headings are often in **bold** type.

3 | Active Previewing

Preview the academic text below. Underline the important words in the title. Read the headings. Then answer the following questions with a partner.

1. What is the first heading? What do you think this section is about?

2. What is the second heading? What do you think this section is about?

3. What is the third heading? What do you think this section is about?

4. How do you think the information in the three sections connects to the title of the passage?

5. What is this text about?

4 | Reading and Recalling

A. Read the text. Stop after each paragraph and tell a partner one thing that you remember about it.

How They Did It: Secrets from FX Experts

The Wolf Man, 1941

1　The theater goes dark, the movie begins, and the audience is waiting expectantly. Anything can happen, especially when a movie has great special effects. Some moviegoers just relax and enjoy the scenes. Others wonder: "How did they do that?" How does a person become an animal? How do people disappear in movies? Where do they get those real-looking dinosaurs? Here are some FX secrets.

2　**Changing**

How do FX specialists turn a person into[1] an animal? For example, in *The Wolf Man* (1941), the main character, played by Lon Chaney Jr., goes outside at night. There's a full moon. Suddenly, his face begins to change. He grows hair and sharp teeth. Now he's a werewolf, a creature that is half-man, half-wolf. How did they do it? To create this effect, makeup artists applied fake hair and teeth to the actor's face. They did this in stages[2]. Here's how: First, with the camera off, the makeup artists applied a little hair and put on slightly longer teeth. Then the camera filmed the actor. The camera turned off again, and the artists put on a little more hair and even longer teeth. They repeated this until the actor's transition[3] to "werewolf" was complete.

continued

---

[1] **turn...into:** cause...to become
[2] **in stages:** gradually; in steps
[3] **transition:** change

continued

3 Disappearing

In many films, characters and objects suddenly disappear. For example, in *The Wizard of Oz* (1939), Dorothy throws water on the Wicked Witch of the West. The witch melts and vanishes in a cloud of steam. Here's how the FX specialists made this happen: Margaret Hamilton, the witch, was actually standing on a small elevator in this scene. It was built into the floor of the set. Her clothes were nailed to the floor. They stayed in place as Hamilton went below the floor on the elevator. Her clothes contained pieces of dry ice (CO_2). Water mixed with CO_2 makes steam, so the witch looked like she was disappearing in a cloud.

The Wizard of Oz, 1939

4 Fantastic Creatures

Dinosaurs, monsters, and imaginary creatures look real and move realistically in many special effect scenes. A good example is in *Jurassic Park* (1993). In one scene, a dinosaur—a Tyrannosaurus rex—attacks a man. To make realistic dinosaurs for *Jurassic Park*, FX specialists studied the work of paleontologists, people who study ancient animals. They learned how dinosaurs really looked and moved. They built models of dinosaurs. They made the models move with hydraulic systems—systems that use the force of water to make machines move. They also used a remote control[4] system called telemetry. These two systems were programmed into a computer. The computers ran[5] the models. This made the dinosaurs' movements seem realistic because they looked the same every time the creatures moved. Some moviegoers are curious about FX secrets; others are not. Either way, good special effects help filmmakers tell stories with imagination, and they enable audiences to experience fantasy.

*Jurassic Park,*1993

---

[4] **remote control:** controlling from a distance
[5] **ran:** made to work

B. Read the text again without stopping. Tell your partner two new pieces of information that you remember.

C. Work as a class or in large groups. Try to say as many things as you can about the text.

5 | Understanding the Text

A. Answer as many questions as you can without looking at the text. Discuss your answers with a partner.

1. What is the text about?

    a. how filmmakers created some famous FX scenes

    b. how filmmakers made some famous movies

    c. how filmmakers make people change or disappear in movies

2. What is the most important idea in each section of the text? Write your answers in the left column below. Then find an example in the text for each section.

What is this section about?	What example does the author give?
Section 1:	
Section 2:	
Section 3:	

B. Answer as many questions as you can without looking at the text. Discuss your answers with a partner.

1. What does a werewolf look like? _____

2. In *The Wizard of Oz*, how does the witch disappear?

    _____

3. In *The Wizard of Oz*, what made the cloud of steam?

    _____

4. In *Jurassic Park*, how did the filmmakers learn about dinosaurs?

    _____

5. How did the filmmakers use computers in *Jurassic Park*?

    _____

6 | Discussing the Issues

Answer the questions and discuss your answers with a partner.

1. Look again at your answers to *Getting Started*, activity *B*, page 29. Were your answers correct?

2. Did any information in the text surprise you? If yes, what surprised you?

3. Discuss other types of FX scenes, such as flying. How do you think filmmakers make people fly in movies?

Putting It On Paper

A. Write a paragraph on one of these topics.

1. Describe your favorite movie. Explain why you like it.

2. Describe your favorite FX scene. Explain why you like it or explain how the filmmakers made it happen.

3. Explain why FX scenes are or are not important in movies.

Steps for your paragraph

a. State the main idea of your paragraph in the first sentence. This is your topic sentence.

b. Include in your paragraph three details that explain your idea.

B. Exchange paragraphs with a partner. Read your partner's paragraph. Answer the questions in the checklist. Give feedback to your partner.

✔ CHECKLIST
1. Is there a clear main idea?
2. Are there enough details?
3. Do all the details connect to the main idea?
4. Write additional comments below.

_____

_____

_____

_____

_____

_____

_____

_____

_____

C. Use your partner's feedback to revise your work.

Taking It Online | Exploring Movies

A. With a partner, use the Internet to find more information about a movie.

ONLINE TIP

Use quotation marks around the title of the movie to get fewer results:
"crouching tiger hidden dragon"
"the matrix"

1. Look for information about a classic movie—an older movie that people still like to watch today—or a new movie. Find out the date the movie appeared, the kind of movie it is, the names of the actors, and any other information that interests you. For example, does the movie have important FX scenes?

2. Use Google (www.google.com) or another major search engine to find sites with the information you want.

3. Preview the sites the same way you would preview a magazine article.

B. Complete the table with the information you find.

Movie
Name of Website:
Website address:
What kind of movie is it?
What year did it appear?
Who are the actors?
What happens in the movie?
Does the movie have FX scenes? If yes, describe one.
Other facts:

C. Following up. Share your facts with your classmates. Make a list of movies that you would like to see.

Sports Psychology

Answer the questions and discuss your answers with a partner.

1. Do you prefer to play sports or watch sports?

2. Look at the photos. Try to name the sports. Which sports are traditional? Which seem new or unusual?

3. Which sports do you like to play? Which sports do you like to watch?

Text 1 | Weird Sports

1 | Getting Started

A. Work with a partner. List as many sports as you can in the chart below. Check (✔) whether you know how to play the sport or not.

I know how to play...	Yes	No
1.	☐	☐
2.	☐	☐
3.	☐	☐
4.	☐	☐
5.	☐	☐
6.	☐	☐
7.	☐	☐
8.	☐	☐
9.	☐	☐
10.	☐	☐

B. Compare your chart with your classmates' charts. Did you learn about any sports that you did not know about before?

2 | Active Previewing

Preview the newspaper quiz on the next page. <u>Underline</u> the important words in the title. Then answer the following question with a partner.

What do you think this text is about?

3 | Reading and Recalling

A. Read the text. Stop after each paragraph and circle your answer. Try not to read the correct answers yet.

The Weird[1] Sports Quiz

How much do you know about sports? Take the quiz and find out. Which sport is real? Which is fake[2]?

1. **Street Luge**[3]: Participants[4] wear motorcycle helmets. They lie on sleds with wheels. (These look like giant skateboards.) They race down city streets at 70 mph.

         Real Sport   Fake Sport

REMEMBER

Skip words that you do not understand. See page 19 for more information on *skipping words*.

2. **Heliboarding:** Snowboarders jump out of a helicopter at the top of a mountain. Then they snowboard down the mountain.

         Real Sport   Fake Sport

3. **Mountain Unicycling:** Bike riders go up and down mountain trails on one-wheeled cycles.

         Real Sport   Fake Sport

4. **Pumpkin[5] Ball:** Players throw pumpkins through basketball hoops.

         Real Sport   Fake Sport

5. **Elephant Polo:** People play polo while they ride on elephants.

         Real Sport   Fake Sport

6. **Curling:** Players slide a large stone (20kg/44lbs) with a broom across an ice rink.

         Real Sport   Fake Sport

7. **Shredding:** Players tear telephone books in half with their bare hands.

         Real Sport   Fake Sport

8. **Carving:** Roller-skating on hard sand on a beach.

         Real Sport   Fake Sport

Correct Answers

1. Real; 2. Fake: Snowboarders DO ride helicopters to the tops of mountains, but they don't jump out of the helicopter; 3. Real; 4. Fake: There is no sport called "Pumpkin Ball"; 5. Real; 6. Real; 7. Fake: "Shredding" is making very difficult surfing moves; 8. Fake: "Carving" means making a long, curving movement while skateboarding.

---

[1] **weird:** strange; unusual

[2] **fake:** not real

[3] **luge:** sled; it slides on smooth surfaces, such as snow

[4] **participants:** people playing or doing the sport

[5] **pumpkin:** a large, round, orange vegetable

B. Read the text again without stopping. This time, read the correct answers. Tell your partner two new pieces of information that you remember.

C. Work as a class or in large groups. Try to say as many things as you can about the text.

4 | Understanding the Text

A. Answer the question without looking at the text. Discuss your answer with a partner.

What is the text about?

    a. a quiz on traditional sports

    b. a quiz on unusual sports

    c. a quiz on sports

B. Take the quiz again in another form. Check (✔) your answers. Then discuss your answers with a partner.

Sport	Real	Fake
1. Carving	☐	☐
2. Curling	☐	☐
3. Elephant Polo	☐	☐
4. Heliboarding	☐	☐
5. Mountain Unicycling	☐	☐
6. Pumpkin Ball	☐	☐
7. Shredding	☐	☐
8. Street Luge	☐	☐

5 | Discussing the Issues

Answer the questions and discuss your answers with a partner.

1. How many answers did you get right the first time?

2. Which "real" sports from the quiz do you know? Do you play or watch any of them?

3. What are some other weird sports?

Text 2 | Skydiving

1 | Getting Started

A. Answer the questions and discuss your answers with a partner.

1. Look at the photo on page 40. What is the person doing?

2. Is skydiving dangerous? Why or why not?

3. Imagine: You are a skydiver. Do *you* think that skydiving is dangerous? How dangerous?

4. Imagine: You are a parent. Your son or daughter is a skydiver. How might you feel about skydiving?

B. Imagine that you are going to interview a skydiver. What questions will you ask? Discuss your questions with a partner.

2 | Skipping Words

A. Read the following sentences from *Text 2*. Check (✔) your guess for the part of speech of the missing word.

1. Kerry Smith met Dave Wheatley, a skydiver on the United States Army parachute xxxx.

    ☐ a. noun   ☐ b. adjective

2. I had a chance to try it, and I xxxxx it.

    ☐ a. noun   ☐ b. verb

3. If I do a good jump, I feel stronger and more xxxxxxxxxx as a person.

    ☐ a. noun   ☐ b. adjective

4. We always say that the wind is our best xxxxxx and our worst enemy.

    ☐ a. noun   ☐ b. adjective

5. Of course, I don't think that parachuting is xxxxxxx.

    ☐ a. noun   ☐ b. adjective

B. Discuss your answers with a partner. Give reasons for your guesses.

3 | Active Previewing

Preview the magazine article on the next page. <u>Underline</u> the important words in the title. Then answer the following question with a partner.

What is this text about?

> **REMEMBER**
>
> Use the important words in the title of a passage to learn what the text is about. See page 2 for more information on *previewing articles*.

A. Read the text. Stop after each paragraph and tell a partner one thing that you remember about it.

Interview with a Skydiver

BY KERRY SMITH

1   Sports writer Kerry Smith met Dave Wheatley, a skydiver on the United States Army parachute team. She asked Dave some questions about his sport.

2 **Q: When did you start skydiving?**
    I started at the age of 23. That was ten years ago.

3 **Q: Why do you like skydiving?**
    I think many people would like to try skydiving. I was lucky. I had a chance to try it, and I liked it.

4   A lot of people think it's exciting, but it's more than that. Every time I do a jump, I improve. If I do a good jump, I feel stronger and more successful as a person. I think skydiving makes me more successful in other parts of my life.

5 **Q: What are the possible dangers of skydiving?**
    The landing is very important. You could land in traffic somewhere. We always say that the wind is our best friend and our worst enemy. It can help us land, or it can make landing very dangerous.

> If I do a good jump, I feel stronger and more successful as a person.

6 **Q: Do you think skydiving is something that you will do for the rest of your life?**
    Yes. I think that most skydivers would agree. I think it stays with you for life. It's a hard thing to put into words[1]. When people ask: "What is skydiving like?", all I can say is, "You can't know until you try it."

7 **Q: Do you think that parachuting is an extreme sport[2]?**
    Of course, I don't think parachuting is extreme. For me, it's something I do every day. But for someone who has an office job, it probably is. My parents definitely think that it's dangerous. Of course, they're proud of me because I'm on the Army parachute team. But my mom doesn't like it; she has been to a couple of shows but never watches me jump.

---

[1] **put into words:** explain clearly
[2] **extreme sport:** a sport that often involves danger, heights, high speed, and so on

B. Read the text again without stopping. Tell your partner two new pieces of information that you remember.

C. Work as a class or in large groups. Try to say as many things as you can about the text.

5 | Understanding the Text

A. Answer the question without looking at the text. Discuss your answer with a partner.

Why did Kerry Smith interview Dave Wheatley?

   a. to find out when he started skydiving

   b. to learn about his experiences as a skydiver

   c. to learn about skydiving

B. Write *T* for *True* or *F* for *False* according to the text. Discuss your answers with a partner.

_____ **1.** Dave started skydiving 23 years ago.

_____ **2.** Dave likes skydiving because it makes him feel lucky.

_____ **3.** Dave says the wind can be both dangerous and helpful.

_____ **4.** Both of Dave's parents often watch him skydive.

_____ **5.** Dave's mom is not happy that Dave is on the Army parachute team.

READING SKILL Understanding the Topic

The **topic** is the subject of a text. The topic is always a word or a phrase. You do not state it as a complete sentence.

When you identify the topic:

1. Choose a word or phrase that best describes the subject of the *whole* text.

2. Do not choose a topic that is too general.

3. Do not choose a topic that is too specific.

Think about *Text 2* on page 24 of Chapter 2. The possible choices for the topic are:

a. a special effects genius

b. the movies of Ray Harryhausen

c. a profile* of Ray Harryhausen

Choice *a* is too general. It does not include something important: the text is a profile on a specific person; that is, it tells about a person's life and accomplishments.

Choice *b* is too specific. It refers only to part of the information about Ray Harryhausen.

Choice *c* is the best topic for the text.

*profile: a story about a person's life

6 | Understanding the Topic

Write *T* for the *Topic* of *Text 2*, *G* for *Too General*, and *S* for *Too Specific*.

1. What is the topic of *Text 2* on page 40?

   a. _____ a skydiver

   b. _____ skydiving

   c. _____ the dangers of skydiving

2. Is your answer for the topic here the same as your answer in *Active Previewing* at the bottom of page 39?

   _____

 VOCABULARY STRATEGY Understanding Subject Pronouns

Pronouns refer to nouns in sentences. We use pronouns to avoid repeating nouns over and over again. A **subject pronoun** replaces a noun that is the subject of a sentence. It replaces a noun that comes *before* it, and it always matches the number (singular or plural) and the gender (*he, she, it*) of the noun that it replaces. The subject pronouns are **I, you, he, she, it, we, you** (plural), and **they**.

Read the following examples.

1. Snowboarders jump out of a helicopter at the top of a mountain. Then *they* snowboard down the mountain.

Who are *they* in the second sentence? *They* are the snowboarders in the first sentence.

2. Curling is a winter sport. *It* is popular in Canada.

What does *it* in the second sentence refer to? *It* refers to *curling* in the first sentence.

7 | Understanding Subject Pronouns

Write the subject that the pronoun refers to in *Text 2* on page 40.

1. She (She asked) (¶1) *Kerry Smith* _____

2. It (It can help) (¶5) _____

3. it (it can make) (¶5) _____

4. they (they're proud) (¶7) _____

5. she (she has been) (¶7) _____

8 | Discussing the Issues

Answer the questions and discuss your answers with a partner.

1. Would you like to skydive? Why or why not?

2. What are some more questions that you could ask Dave Wheatley? List them.

3. Think about an athlete in another sport. What are some good interview questions for him or her?

Text 3 | Sports Injuries

1 | Getting Started

Answer the questions and discuss your answers with a partner.

1. Look at your list of sports in *Getting Started*, page 36. Which are safe? Which are dangerous? Give your opinion.

2. Do you have any extreme sports on your list? If not, add some.

3. Are traditional sports usually safe? Why or why not? Give examples.

4. Are extreme sports usually dangerous? Why or why not? Give examples.

2 | Active Previewing

Preview the table on page 45 and then answer the questions. Discuss your answers with a partner.

1. What is the title of the table? Underline the important words.

2. What words are in the top row of the table?

_____

_____

3. What kind of information is in the left-hand column? Give three examples.

_____

_____

4. What is the table about?

    a. the number of injuries for certain sports

    b. the number of players for certain sports

    c. the number of injuries for extreme sports

Scanning is looking for information quickly before or after you read a text. You often scan for numbers, especially in tables. Tables often list numbers in *percents. Percents* are numbers that show how an amount relates to 100. They help you quickly compare things.

Read the table and the question below.

Sport	Safe	Dangerous
Paintball	25%	75%
Basketball	75%	25%

Which sport do most people think is safer, basketball or paintball?

The table presents the results of a study: 75 people out of 100 said that paintball is a dangerous sport; 25 people out of 100 said that basketball is a dangerous sport. The percentages in the table help you to answer the question. You can quickly see that most people think that basketball is safer than paintball.

3 | Scanning Tables

Scan the table on page 45 to find the answers to the questions. Discuss your answers with a partner.

1. Which sports are extreme? _____

2. Which sport has the most participants? _____

3. Which sport has the most injuries? _____

4. Which sport has the lowest number of injuries? _____

5. Which sport has the highest percentage of injuries per total number of participants?

   _____

6. Which sport has the lowest percentage of injuries per total number of participants?

   _____

7. Which sport seems the safest, according to this table? _____

Sports Injuries[1]

The chart below shows sports injuries in one country in one year. It shows traditional sports and extreme sports (**in bold**). Experts show sports injuries this way: they count the number of injuries among the total number of participants in one year.

Sport	Number of Participants	Number of Injuries	Percent (%) of Injuries per Number of Participants
Basketball	36,584	2,783	7.6
Bixling (BMX)	3,885	188	5.3
Football	5,783	1,084	18.8
Martial Arts	5,996	610	10.2
Mountain Climbing	6,000	337	5.6
Paintball	5,000	1	.02
Skateboarding	12,997	289	3.1
Snowboarding	7,691	218	2.8
Soccer[2]	17,641	1,634	9.3
Surfing	1,879	99	5.3
Tennis	16,353	415	2.5
Wrestling	2,026	133	9.0

Note: Distances are estimates.[3]

---

[1] **injuries:** plural of *injury*; damage to the body

[2] **soccer:** the American name for *football*

[3] **estimates:** numbers that are not exact, but close to exact

4 | Discussing the Issues

Answer the questions and discuss your answers with a partner.

1. Do you play any of the sports in the table? If yes, which ones?

2. Which information in the table surprises you? Give examples.

3. How can people try to avoid injuries when they play dangerous sports?

Text 4 | Taking Risks in Sports

1 | Getting Started

A. Think about your answers to the questions in the chart. Then fill in the chart with information from three classmates.

Questions	Name _____	Name _____	Name _____
1. Do you like to do dangerous things (for example, drive a car fast)? Why or why not?			
2. If you answered *yes* to question *1*, give examples of dangerous things that you like to do. If you answered *no*, explain why you do NOT like to do dangerous things.			
3. Do you like to take chances? (For example, do you like to gamble—play games for money?) Why or why not?			
4. If you answered *yes* to question *3*, give examples of chances that you take. If you answered *no*, explain why you do NOT take chances.			

B. Discuss your chart with a partner. Then answer the following questions.

1. How many people like to do dangerous things?

2. How many like to take chances?

3. What kinds of things do they do? Why do they do them?

You can preview a text by **making predictions**—thinking about what the text is about *before* you read it.

To make predictions:

1. Look at the title and any headings. The title and headings often tell you the important ideas in the text.

2. Guess what the author of the text might say about these ideas.

Re-read the title and headings from *Text 4* of Chapter 2:

Title: How They Did It: Secrets from FX Experts

Headings: Changing • Disappearing • Fantastic Creatures

You can guess: The author might give information about how FX experts make special effects. The author will probably explain three types of FX: changing, disappearing, and fantastic creatures. The author will probably give examples of movies with these types of FX.

These predictions will help you understand the text.

2 | Active Previewing

Preview the academic text on the next page. <u>Underline</u> the important words in the title. Read the headings. Make predictions. Then answer the following questions with a partner.

1. What is this text about? _____

2. What are the important ideas in the text? _____

3. What kind of information will the author probably give? Write at least three ideas.

_____

_____

4. What is the text about?

a. risk-takers

b. the psychology of risk-taking

c. extreme sports

A. Read the text. Stop after each paragraph. Tell a partner one thing that you remember about it.

High-Risk Sports

1 We all take risks every day. For example, we take risks when we cross the street, ask someone for a date, or ask the teacher a question that we think is "stupid." These are everyday risks—actions that have uncertain results. However, some risks are extreme. For example, participating in dangerous sports such as mountain climbing and skydiving can be extremely risky. Why do some people like extreme or dangerous sports? Do they want to hurt themselves? Or is there some other reason? Psychologists are people who study human behavior, and some psychologists study risk behavior. These experts might have some of the answers.

2 **Who Is a Risk-Taker?**

Today, a risk-taker is a person who participates in an action that has possible danger or an uncertain result. Experts have some facts about risk-takers, and they also have some guesses about them. They know these facts: Young males are the most likely to be risk-takers, and people become less interested in risk-taking as they get older. In addition, some people still feel the need or desire to take risks. Many experts guess this: Risk-taking was important for our ancestors[1]. It helped them to fight and to find food. It helped them to survive. Therefore, it helped them to evolve into[2] modern humans.

3 There are positive and negative results of risk-taking. Risk takers are often more successful than non-risk-takers: Inventors, politicians, and CEOs—people who lead companies—are often risk-takers. However, risk-takers may also become bored easily and become unhappy with their lives.

4 **The Sports Risk-Taker**

People who take sports risks have certain personality characteristics. Like other risk takers, they are usually male and they usually have a group of friends like them. Generally, they are very confident people. They have calm personalities; that is, they do not usually feel anxiety.

continued

---

[1] **ancestors:** early humans; people who lived a long time ago

[2] **evolve into:** become

Usually, they like dangerous sports because they need much more stimulation[3] than other people do. When they do extreme sports, they usually believe that they are in control of the situation. Also, they feel excitement instead of fear.

5 **One Type of Sports Risk-Taker: The Mountain Climber**

A researcher studied one group of high-risk athletes—mountain climbers. He asked them about themselves. Here's what they said: They climb because it makes them feel good about themselves. They climb because it makes them feel alive. They climb because it helps them to learn things about themselves. Many of these climbers also say this: they are addicted[4]. They cannot stop, even after accidents.

6 An example is Jim Wickwire. He climbed to the top of Pakistan's 28,250-foot (8,610 meters) K-2, the second highest mountain peak in the world. On K-2, Wickwire lost several of his toes because he had frostbite, a condition in which freezing injures the skin. He also lost half a lung because he got altitude sickness (a sickness that comes from not having enough oxygen). He even saw many climbing partners fall thousands of feet and then die. Did Wickwire stop climbing? No. He still climbs, even though he is not sure why.

7 To some experts, extreme risk taking is not normal. To other experts, risk taking is an important part of being successful. What do you think?

---

[3] **stimulation:** something that gives excitement and/or increases activity

[4] **addicted:** dependent; not able to stop

B. Read the text again without stopping. Tell your partner two new pieces of information that you remember.

C. Work as a class or in large groups. Try to name as many things as you can about the text.

4 | Understanding the Topic

Write *T* for the *Topic* of *Text 4*, *G* for *Too General*, and *S* for *Too Specific*.

1. What is the topic of *Text 4*?

    a. _____ why people take risks in sports

    b. _____ why people do certain things

    c. _____ why mountain climbers take risks

2. Is your answer for the topic here the same as your answer in *Active Previewing* on page 47?

5 | Understanding the Text

A. Complete as many items as you can without looking at the text. Discuss your answers with a partner.

1. An example of an everyday risk is

    a. climbing a mountain.

    b. crossing the street.

    c. skydiving.

2. Why was risk-taking important to early humans?

    a. It helped them live long lives.

    b. It helped them to survive in cold weather.

    c. It helped them to stay alive.

3. Which of the following is true about risk-takers?

    a. They are often successful people.

    b. They are often happy people.

    c. They are often healthy people.

4. A researcher studied mountain climbers because

    a. they do not like to take risks.

    b. climbing makes them feel good about themselves.

    c. they participate in a high-risk sport.

5. What is Jim Wickwire an example of?

    a. a mountain climber

    b. a person who is addicted to mountain climbing

    c. a mountain climber who has a lot of accidents

6. What has Jim Wickwire lost while climbing?

    a. several of his toes

    b. half a lung

    c. climbing partners

    d. all of the above

B. Check (✔) the characteristics of a risk-taker. Try not to look back at the text. Discuss your answers with a partner.

Risk-takers usually...
☐ 1. are female.
☐ 2. are confident.
☐ 3. have friends who are like them.
☐ 4. feel anxiety.
☐ 5. need more stimulation than others.
☐ 6. believe that they are in control.
☐ 7. feel excitement, not fear.
☐ 8. are older.

VOCABULARY STRATEGY Understanding Vocabulary in Context— Definitions

Sometimes you can understand new words or expressions from a **definition** in the text. The definition might be in the same sentence or in the next sentence. Definitions usually follow words such as *is*, *are*, or *means*. Some definitions follow commas (,) or dashes (—). Sometime definitions are inside parentheses ( ).

Read this sentence from *Text 4*:

A *risk-taker* is a person who participates in an action that has a possible danger or an uncertain result.

If you do not know the word *risk-taker*, you can guess because there is a definition after *is* (*a person who participates in an action that has a possible danger or an uncertain result*).

6 | Understanding Vocabulary in Context—Definitions

Read the following sentences from *Text 4.* **Check (✔) the part of speech for the underlined words and expressions. Then write their definitions on the lines.**

1. These are everyday <u>risks</u>—actions that have uncertain results.

    ☐ a. noun ☐ b. verb ☐ c. adjective

    _____

2. <u>Psychologists</u> are people who study human behavior.

    ☐ a. noun ☐ b. verb ☐ c. adjective

    _____

3. <u>CEOs</u>—people who lead companies—are often risk-takers.

    ☐ a. noun ☐ b. verb ☐ c. adjective

    _____

4. On K-2, Wickwire lost several of his toes because he had <u>frostbite</u>, a condition in which freezing injures the skin.

    ☐ a. noun ☐ b. verb ☐ c. adjective

    _____

5. He also lost half a lung because he got <u>altitude sickness</u> (a sickness that comes from not having enough oxygen).

    ☐ a. noun ☐ b. verb ☐ c. adjective

    _____

7 | Discussing the Issues

Answer the questions and discuss your answers with a partner.

1. Is extreme risk-taking normal? Why or why not?

2. Mountain climbers take risks because it makes them feel alive and good about themselves. What are some less dangerous ways to help you feel good about yourself?

3. Mountain climbers like Jim Wickwire can become addicted to their sport. Is this a bad thing? Can some addictions be good? Explain.

Putting It On Paper

A. Write a paragraph on one of these topics.

1. Describe your favorite sport. Explain how to play it or why it is your favorite.

2. Is risk-taking normal behavior? Why or why not?

Steps for your paragraph

a. State the main idea of your paragraph in the first sentence. This is your topic sentence.

b. Include in your paragraph three details that explain your idea.

B. Exchange paragraphs with a partner. Read your partner's paragraph. Answer the questions in the checklist. Give feedback to your partner.

✔ CHECKLIST
1. Is there a clear main idea?
2. Are there enough details?
3. Do all the details connect to the main idea?
4. Write additional comments below.

_____

_____

_____

_____

_____

_____

_____

_____

_____

_____

C. Use your partner's feedback to revise your work.

Taking It Online | Exploring Sports

A. With a partner, use the Internet to find more information about sports.

1. Choose a sport that you want to learn more about. It can be a traditional sport, a weird sport, or an extreme sport. Find out about the history of the sport, how people play it, what equipment they need to play it (for example, balls, roller-skates, and so on), and anything else that interests you.

2. Use Google (www.google.com) or another major search engine to find sites with the information you want.

3. Preview the sites as you would a magazine article.

ONLINE TIP

Combine key words:
elephant polo + rules
snowboarding + history
paintball + equipment

B. Complete the chart with the information you find.

Sport
Type of sport:
Name of Website:
Website address:
When did people first start playing this sport?
Where do people play this sport?
What equipment do people need?
How do you play this sport?
What type of people usually play this sport?
Other facts:

C. Following up. Share your facts with your classmates. Which sport is the most unusual? Which sport would be the most fun? Which sport might be the most dangerous?

Chapter 4

The Culture of Music

READING SKILLS

- Previewing First Sentences, page 60
- Understanding the Main Idea, page 70

VOCABULARY STRATEGY

- Understanding Vocabulary in Context—Examples, page 59

GRAPHICS

- Understanding Tables, page 66

Answer the questions and discuss your answers with a partner.

1. How often do you listen to music?

2. Look at the photos. Which kinds of music do you know? Which kinds do you listen to?

3. What is your favorite kind of music?

Text 1 | Favorite Music

1 | Getting Started

A. Work with a partner. List as many kinds of music as you can. Check (✔) the kinds that you like. Then ask your partner which kinds he or she likes.

Kinds of music	I like it.	My partner likes it.
1.	☐	☐
2.	☐	☐
3.	☐	☐
4.	☐	☐
5.	☐	☐
6.	☐	☐
7.	☐	☐
8.	☐	☐
9.	☐	☐

B. Compare your chart with the others in the class. Then answer the following questions and discuss them with your partner.

1. What is the most popular kind of music?

2. What is the least popular kind?

2 | Active Previewing

Preview the newspaper article on the next page. <u>Underline</u> the important words in the title. Make predictions. Then answer the following questions with a partner.

1. What do you think this text is about?

2. What kind of information will it have?

3 | Reading and Recalling

A. Read the text. Stop after each paragraph and tell a partner one thing that you remember about it.

What's Your Favorite Kind of Music?

BY MILES JONES

1 Today, our question is: What's your favorite kind of music?

2 **Helen, 45, college professor:** I love rock, especially oldies[1] such as the Beatles and the Rolling Stones. I don't like the pop[2] groups of today very much, though.

3 **Danielle, 13, student (Helen's daughter):** My favorite type of music is rock, too. I like the same stuff that my mom likes, but I like cool stuff, too. Like, I have Green Day and The White Stripes on my iPod®. Wanna listen?

4 **Marcus, 22, college student:** I like jazz and classical music. I'm an art major, and I listen to music while I work. Jazz and classical music inspire me[3]; they help me to think and to be creative.

5 **Pat, 33, musician:** I perform in the local symphony orchestra, so of course, I love classical music. I play the violin in the orchestra, but I play all kinds of stringed instruments. I love to listen to string ensembles[4] like the Eroica Trio.

6 **Rob, 21, waiter:** My favorite type of music is world music. I like music from lots of cultures. I like music from the Caribbean, especially reggae. I also like music from Latin America, like salsa and Asian fusion. That's traditional Asian music mixed with modern music.

7 **Chris, 27, computer graphics designer:** I like just about every kind of music. I love hip-hop and rap—that's what I listen to at work. The only kinds of music I absolutely do *not* like are country music and opera. I can't listen to them!

---

[1] **oldies:** older popular music—for example, from the 1960s, 1970s, or the 1980s

[2] **pop:** popular music

[3] **inspire me:** encourage me

[4] **ensembles:** small groups of musicians

B. Read the text again without stopping. Tell your partner two new pieces of information that you remember.

C. Work as a class or in small groups. Try to say as many things as you can about the text.

4 | Understanding the Topic

Write *T* for the *Topic* of *Text 1*, *G* for *Too General*, and *S* for *Too Specific*.

1. What is the topic of *Text 1*?

   a. _____ opinions

   b. _____ opinions about pop music

   c. _____ some people's opinions about music

2. Is your answer for the topic here the same as your answer in *Active Previewing* on page 56?

   _____

5 | Understanding the Text

A. Answer as many questions as you can without looking at the text. Discuss your answers with a partner.

1. What do Helen and her daughter Danielle agree on?

   a. They both like rock music.

   b. They both do not like modern rock groups.

   c. They both like The White Stripes.

2. What does Marcus listen to while he works?

   a. jazz

   b. jazz and classical

   c. opera

3. The Eroica Trio is an example of a

   a. jazz ensemble.

   b. stringed instrument.

   c. string ensemble.

4. What is "Asian fusion"?

   a. Latin American music mixed with modern music

   b. Caribbean music mixed with traditional Asian music

   c. traditional Asian music mixed with modern music

5. What does Chris listen to at work?

   a. hip-hop and rap

   b. every kind of music

   c. opera and country music

B. Match the opinions about music with the people in the interview. Discuss your answers with a partner. There can be more than one person for some opinions.

Opinions about music	Person
_____ 1. doesn't like opera	a. Helen, college professor
_____ 2. likes classical music	b. Danielle, Helen's daughter
_____ 3. likes jazz	c. Marcus, college student
_____ 4. likes music from different cultures	d. Pat, musician
_____ 5. likes oldies	e. Rob, waiter
_____ 6. likes rock	f. Chris, computer graphics designer

 VOCABULARY STRATEGY Understanding Vocabulary in Context— Examples

Examples can explain new words in a text. Examples often follow phrases like *for example, such as, especially,* and *like,* or sometimes they follow a colon (:). They can be in the same sentence as the new word or in another sentence.

Read the following sentences:

1. I love rock, especially *oldies* such as the Beatles and the Rolling Stones.

What are *oldies*? *Such as* tells us that *oldies* means music from rock groups *such as the Beatles and the Rolling Stones.*

Sometimes the example is the new word. In this case, the information that comes before the new word explains it.

2. I also like music from Latin America—like *salsa.*

What is *salsa*? *Salsa* is *music from Latin America.*

6 | Understanding Vocabulary in Context—Examples

Use examples from *Text 1* on page 57 to help you write the meaning of each word or phrase.

1. stringed instruments (¶5) _____

2. string ensembles (¶5) _____

3. reggae (¶6) _____

7 | Discussing the Issues

Answer the questions and discuss your answers with a partner.

1. How does your favorite kind of music make you feel?

2. Who are your favorite musicians? Who are your favorite musical groups? Who are your favorite singers?

3. What kind of music do you *not* like? Why don't you like it?

Text 2 | Earth Harp

1 | Getting Started

A. Answer the questions and discuss your answers with a partner.

1. What is your favorite instrument?

2. Do you play an instrument? If yes, which one(s)? Do you play for yourself or for other people?

3. List as many stringed instruments as you can. Explain how musicians play them.

B. Discuss with the class your answer to number *3* above. How many stringed instruments are there? Can any of your classmates explain how to play each of them?

 READING SKILL Previewing First Sentences

You can **preview** a text by reading **the first sentence** of each paragraph. First sentences often (but not always) tell you what the paragraph is about. Like the title and the headings, first sentences can tell you the most important ideas in the text.

Read the following first sentences from *Text 4* of Chapter 3 on page 48:

1. There are positive and negative results of risk-taking. (¶3)

2. People who take sports risks have certain personality characteristics. (¶4)

Previewing the first sentences tells you:

In ¶3, the author will probably discuss the positive and negative results of risk-taking.

In ¶4, the author will probably discuss the characteristics of sports risk-takers.

You can see how much information you can learn about a text just by previewing first sentences.

2 | Active Previewing

Preview the magazine article below. <u>Underline</u> the important words in the title. Read the first sentence of each paragraph. Make predictions. Then answer the following questions with a partner.

1. What do you think this text is about?

2. What are the important ideas in the text?

3. What kind of information will the author probably give? List at least three things.

3 | Reading and Recalling

A. Read the text. Stop after each paragraph. Tell a partner one thing that you remember about it.

The Earth Harp: The World's Largest Stringed Instrument

Close's Earth Harp

1   Imagine a giant stringed musical instrument: it's over 1,100 feet high and 80 feet long. Now, imagine the player of the instrument: She hangs upside down, inside the instrument. A belt

Andrea Brooks playing the Earth Harp

attaches her to it. She gently moves her fingers across the strings of the instrument with gloved hands. The player is like an acrobat. She moves just like a circus entertainer as she spins around and rubs other strings. The instrument makes a loud, thunderous sound.

2   This is an Earth Harp. The player is Andrea Brooks, and her husband, Bill Close, invented the instrument. A long time ago, Close read this quote by the American architect[1] Frank Lloyd

continued

---

[1] **architect:** a person who designs buildings

Wright: "Architecture[2] is frozen music." This idea inspired him to combine architecture and music and invent new instruments.

3   Just one of Close's instruments can make the sound of an entire string section—many stringed instruments playing together. _____ Close builds these giant harps in many places. He sets them up out-doors or in theatres. Close likes to combine parts of the instrument with the environment. Outside, in a plaza[3], for example, the harp strings can travel across the open space and attach to surrounding buildings. Close also likes to include the people who are listening. For example, in theatres, the strings sometimes go over the

> Close likes to combine parts of the instrument with the environment.

heads of the audience and attach to the back wall. This way, the audience members feel like they are inside the harp.

4   Close performs with his wife and his team, the MASS (Music Architecture Sonic Sculpture) ensemble. They play the giant stringed instruments, along with traditional instruments such as violins, cellos, flutes, and drums. They also play other invented instruments. Some of the team members dance as they play. MASS performs many types of music—including pop and classical music—at many venues, including theatres, museums, and open spaces around the United States and Mexico.

---

[2] **architecture:** the study or practice of designing buildings
[3] **plaza:** an open space in a city or town

B. Read the text again without stopping. Tell your partner two new pieces of information that you remember.

C. Work as a class or in large groups. Try to name as many things as you can about the text.

4 | Understanding the Topic

Write *T* for the Topic of *Text 2*, *G* for *Too General*, and *S* for *Too Specific*.

1. What is the topic of *Text 2*?

    a. _____ invented instruments

    b. _____ an inventor of instruments

    c. _____ the Earth Harp

2. Is your answer for the topic here the same as your answer in *Active Previewing* on page 61?

_____

5 | Understanding the Text

A. Complete as many sentences as you can without looking at the text. Discuss your answers with a partner.

1. The Earth Harp is

    a. over 80 feet high.

    b. over 1,100 feet high.

    c. over 1,100 feet long.

2. The player of the Earth Harp

    a. plays it as she moves around the inside of the instrument.

    b. plays it as she climbs around the outside of the instrument.

    c. plays it as she stands next to the instrument.

3. The player plays the Earth Harp

    a. with her feet.

    b. with a belt.

    c. with her fingers.

4. The inventor of the Earth Harp is

    a. Frank Lloyd Wright.

    b. Bill Close.

    c. Andrea Brooks.

5. To invent the Earth Harp, the inventor combined

    a. architecture and dance.

    b. architecture and acrobatics.

    c. architecture and music.

6. MASS preforms at many venues, including

    a. theatres.

    b. museums.

    c. open spaces.

    d. all of the above.

B. Check (✔) the facts from the text about the Earth Harp. Discuss your answers with a partner.

☐ 1. The Earth Harp is very quiet.

☐ 2. The player of the Earth Harp is the inventor's husband.

☐ 3. The Earth Harp can only be played outside.

☐ 4. The inventor of the Earth Harp invents other kinds of instruments.

☐ 5. The MASS ensemble plays invented instruments with traditional instruments.

☐ 6. The MASS ensemble combines dance with their performances.

☐ 7. The MASS ensemble does not play popular music.

6 | Understanding Vocabulary in Context

A. Synonyms. Read the following sentences from *Text 2*. Check (✔) the part of speech of the underlined words.

1. The player is like an <u>acrobat</u>. She moves just like a circus entertainer as she spins around and rubs other strings.

☐ a. noun   ☐ b. verb   ☐ c. adjective

2. The instrument makes a loud, <u>thunderous</u> sound.

☐ a. noun   ☐ b. verb   ☐ c. adjective

3. Close likes to combine parts of the instrument with the <u>environment</u>. Outside, in a plaza, for example, the harp strings can travel across the open space and attach to surrounding buildings.

☐ a. noun   ☐ b. verb   ☐ c. adjective

B. Definitions. Now write definitions for the synonyms on the lines below.

1. acrobat _____

_____

2. thunderous _____

_____

3. environment _____

_____

7 | Understanding Vocabulary in Context—Examples

Use examples from *Text 2* on pages 61–62 to help you write the meaning of each word or phrase.

1. the environment (¶3) _____

   _____

2. audience (¶3) _____

   _____

3. traditional instruments (¶4) _____

   _____

4. venues (¶4) _____

   _____

8 | Understanding Subject Pronouns

Write the subject that the pronoun refers to in *Text 2*.

1. she (she spins) (¶1) _____

2. He (He sets them up) (¶3) _____

3. They (They play) (¶4) _____

4. They (They also play) (¶4) _____

> **REMEMBER**
> A subject pronoun replaces a noun that is the subject of a sentence. See page 42 for more on *subject pronouns*.

9 | Discussing the Issues

Answer the questions and discuss your answers with a partner.

1. What do you think Frank Lloyd Wright meant when he said, "Architecture is frozen music"? What does it mean to Bill Close?

2. Why do you think Bill Close named his instrument the "Earth Harp"?

3. What are some other ways people combine art with the environment? Are there other kinds of art that include the audience? If yes, give examples.

Text 3 | Hit Songs

1 | Getting Started

Answer the questions and discuss your answers with a partner.

1. Make a list of pop singers and musicians who are very popular around the world. Think of people from the past and the present.

2. What's your favorite pop song? Do you think that many people agree?

3. Guess: What would people say is their favorite pop song?

 GRAPHICS Understanding Tables

> **Tables** show statistics in different ways. In Chapters 2 and 3, you previewed tables with top-row and left-hand column headings. Some tables do not have left-hand column headings. To preview these tables, look at the title and the top-row headings.

2 | Active Previewing

Preview the table on the next page. Then answer the questions. Discuss your answers with a partner.

1. What is the title of the table? _____

2. What words are in the top row of the table? _____

3. What is the topic of the table? _____

> **REMEMBER**
> Preview tables by looking at the title, especially the important words. Then look at the top-row headings. See page 26 for more information on *previewing tables*.

3 | Scanning Tables

Scan the table on page 67 to find the answers to the questions. Discuss your answers with a partner.

1. Who sang "Diana"? _____

2. How many millions of units did "It's Now or Never" sell? _____

3. What songs in the table did the Beatles record? _____

4. Which songs sold the same number of units? _____

5. Which artists in the list have the same rank in the list? _____

6. How many Elvis Presley songs are there in the table?

_____

7. Which artist(s) in the chart recorded the song with the lowest number of sales?

_____

8. Which song sold the most units?

_____

REMEMBER

When you scan a table, do not look at everything. Move your eyes quickly. Just look for the information that you need. See page 44 for more information on _scanning tables_.

The Top Ten Selling Singles[1] in the World

Following are the all-time best selling hit singles in millions[2] of units sold:

RANK[3]	SONG TITLE	ARTIST[4]	GLOBAL SALES (MILLIONS)
1	Candle in the Wind '97	Elton John	37
2	White Christmas	Bing Crosby	30
3	Rock Around the Clock	Bill Haley	17
4	I Want to Hold Your Hand	The Beatles	12
5	Hey Jude	The Beatles	10
5	It's Now or Never	Elvis Presley	10
5	I Will Always Love You	Whitney Houston	10
8	Hound Dog	Elvis Presley	9
8	Diana	Paul Anka	9
10	I'm a Believer	The Monkees	8
10	(Everything I Do) I Do It For You	Bryan Adams	8

[1] **singles:** songs that are individually recorded

[2] **units:** individual items

[3] **rank:** position; place

[4] **artist:** performer

4 | Discussing the Issues

Answer the questions and discuss your answers with a partner.

1. Do you know any of the songs in the table? If yes, which ones?

2. Did any of the information in the table surprise you? Give examples.

3. Can you explain why any of these ten songs or artists are so popular?

Text 4 | Hip-Hop Music

1 | Getting Started

A. Answer the questions and discuss your answers with a partner.

1. What countries or cultures are most famous for these types of music: jazz, hip-hop, rock, reggae?

2. Do you like hip-hop and rap music? Why or why not?

3. Can you name some hip-hop or rap artists? If yes, which ones?

B. Write _T_ next to things that are _True_ about hip-hop. Write _F_ next to things that are _False_. Work in small groups.

_____ 1. Hip-hop started in New York City.

_____ 2. One of the first hip-hop recordings was called "Rapper's Delight."

_____ 3. An immigrant from Africa started the hip-hop musical style.

_____ 4. Hip-hop started in the 1980s.

_____ 5. Rapping means playing two records at the same time.

2 | Active Previewing

Preview the academic text on the next page. <u>Underline</u> the important words in the title. Read the headings. Read the first sentence of each paragraph. Make predictions. Then answer the following questions with a partner.

1. What is this text about?

2. What are the important ideas in the text?

3. What kind of information will the author probably give? Name at least three things.

> **REMEMBER**
> Use the important words in the title of a passage and in the headings to make predictions. See page 47 for more information on *making predictions.*

3 | Reading and Recalling

A. Read the text. Stop after each paragraph and tell a partner one thing that you remember about it.

The History of Hip-Hop

1   Hip-hop is both a culture and a style of pop music. As a style of music, hip-hop includes *rapping* (or *MC-ing*) and *DJ-ing*. Rapping is speaking or singing rhyming words to music. DJ-ing is mixing sections from two or more records and/or scratching[1] the records while they play. Hip-hop also includes an acrobatic dance style called *breakdancing*.

Breakdancing

The Birth of Hip-Hop

When people think about the beginnings of hip-hop music, they often think of the song "Rapper's Delight." The Sugar Hill Gang recorded it in 1979. In fact, "Rapper's Delight" *was* one of the first hip-hop numbers ever recorded. However, hip-hop actually started almost ten years before.

3   Hip-hop was born in the South Bronx (New York City) in the early 1970s. Originally, it was a live performance art. It wasn't recorded. People performed hip-hop in clubs and at parties, and especially outdoors—for example, in parks.

DJ Cool Herc (*on right*)

Many hip-hop historians agree that DJ Cool Herc is the father of hip-hop. In fact, DJ Cool Herc invented most of the performance styles that we call "hip-hop" today.

4 Hip-Hop's Jamaican Roots

DJ Cool Herc was born in Jamaica. (His real name is Clive Campbell.) He came to the United States in 1967, and his family lived in the Bronx. When DJ Cool Herc was a child in Jamaica, he listened to reggae music. People drove vans with loud sound systems around the towns and cities and broadcasted[2] reggae music. This was a popular kind of entertainment because many Jamaicans didn't have their own stereo systems.

5   DJ Cool Herc loved the music vans of Jamaica. They gave him an idea. He set up a sound system in the basement of his family's apartment in the Bronx and started DJ-ing on his sound system. Herc specialized in finding very rhythmic[3] sections of records. When he played these, it made people want to dance. These breaks—sections on the records—started a new type of dancing called "breakdancing."

6   Later, while he was performing at a club, Herc invented the "merry-go-round." With the merry-go-round, Herc put two records on separate turntables at the same time. He went back

continued

---

[1] **scratching:** rubbing with something sharp in a way that makes additional noise

[2] **broadcasted:** sent out; transmitted

[3] **rhythmic:** having a regular sound pattern; with a beat

continued

and forth between the two records and played the rhythm breaks on each one. This created long sessions of danceable music.

7 The Beginnings of Rapping

Herc also shouted out to the audience. He encouraged[4] them to dance. This shouting also came from Jamaica. In Jamaica, it's called "toasting." In Jamaica, an MC rode in the sound-system van and shouted out to the listeners. Herc's shouting was the beginning of rapping, the rhyming chants[5] that go with hip-hop music.

8   Many other musicians in the Bronx copied Herc and added to his inventions. Some of these were Afrika Bambaataa (Kevin Donovan) and Grandmaster Flash (Joseph Saddler). They all contributed to the musical and cultural style called hip-hop.

---

[4] **encouraged:** suggested strongly; persuaded

[5] **chants:** rhythmic songs in which many words and phrases are repeated

B. Read the text again without stopping. Tell your partner two new pieces of information that you remember.

C. Work as a class or in large groups. Try to name as many things as you can about the text.

READING SKILL Understanding the Main Idea

The **main idea** of a text is the most important idea that the writer wants to say about the topic. You always state the main idea as a complete sentence.

When you identify the main idea:

1. Choose the idea that best describes the most important idea of the *whole* text.

2. Do not choose a main idea that is too general.

3. Do not choose a main idea that is too specific.

Think about *Text 4* on pages 48–49 of Chapter 3.

The possible choices for the main idea are:

a. There are many kinds of risk-takers.

b. Mountain climbers have certain risk-taking characteristics.

c. People who take sports risks have certain characteristics.

Choice *a* is too general. It does not include something important: The text is about people who take risks in sports.

Choice *b* is too specific. Mountain climbers are only one type of sports risk-taker.

Choice *c* is the best main idea for *Text 4*.

4 | Understanding the Topic and the Main Idea

Write *T* for the *Topic*, *G* for *Too General*, and *S* for *Too Specific*. Discuss your answers with a partner.

1. What is the topic of *Text 4* on pages 69–70?

   a. _____ the history of hip-hop

   b. _____ the history of one type of pop music

   c. _____ the Jamaican characteristics of hip-hop

2. What is the main idea of *Text 4*?

   a. _____ Some popular musical styles have many influences.

   b. _____ Hip-hop is a musical style with many influences.

   c. _____ DJ Cool Herc started the musical style called hip-hop.

5 | Understanding the Text

A. Complete as many sentences as you can without looking at the text. Discuss your answers with a partner.

1. Hip-hop is

   a. a musical style.

   b. a cultural style.

   c. a cultural and musical style.

2. Hip-hop was born in

   a. the early 70s.

   b. the late 60s.

   c. 1979.

3. DJ Cool Herc got the idea for hip-hop from

   a. music clubs in the Bronx.

   b. the music vans of Jamaica.

   c. records that his family played.

4. "Rhythm breaks" are

   a. chants that accompany hip-hop music.

   b. scratched sections of records.

   c. sections of danceable music on records.

5. Rapping is

   a. the chanting that goes with hip-hop music.

   b. the record-scratching that goes with hip-hop music.

   c. the dancing that goes with hip-hop music.

B. Answer the questions in *Getting Started*, part *B*, on page 68 again. Correct any incorrect statements.

6 | Understanding Vocabulary in Context—Definitions

Read the following sentences from *Text 4*. Check (✔) the part of speech for the underlined words and expressions. Then write their definitions on the lines.

REMEMBER

Look for definitions after *is, are, means,* a comma, or a dash. See page 51 for more on *definitions*.

1. <u>Hip-hop</u> is both a culture and a style of pop music.

   ☐ a. noun   ☐ b. verb   ☐ c. adjective

   _____

2. <u>Rapping</u> is speaking or singing rhyming words to music.

   ☐ a. noun   ☐ b. verb   ☐ c. adjective

   _____

3. <u>DJ-ing</u> is mixing sections from two or more records and/or scratching the records while they play.

   ☐ a. noun   ☐ b. verb   ☐ c. adjective

   _____

4. Hip-hop also includes an acrobatic dance style called <u>breakdancing</u>.

   ☐ a. noun   ☐ b. verb   ☐ c. adjective

   _____

7 | Understanding Subject Pronouns

Write the subject that the pronoun refers to in *Text 4*.

1. they (they often think) (¶2) _____

2. it (Originally, it was) (¶3) _____

3. He (He came to) (¶4) _____

4. it's (In Jamaica, it's called) (¶7) _____

8 | Discussing the Issues

Answer the questions and discuss your answers with a partner.

1. Think of examples of current music that include some of Herc's hip-hop inventions.

2. What are some musical styles that have influences from different cultures?

3. Some people say that music is a universal language—a language that anyone in the world can understand. Do you agree? Explain your answer.

Putting It On Paper

A. Write a paragraph on one of these topics.

1. Describe your favorite kind of music. Explain why it is your favorite.

2. Is music a universal language? Explain your answer.

Steps for your paragraph

    a. State the main idea of your paragraph in the first sentence. This is your topic sentence.

    b. Include in your paragraph three details that explain your idea.

B. Exchange paragraphs with a partner. Read your partner's paragraph. Answer the questions in the checklist. Give feedback to your partner.

✔ CHECKLIST
1. Is there a clear main idea?
2. Are there enough details?
3. Do all the details connect to the main idea?
4. Write additional comments below.

_____

_____

_____

_____

_____

_____

_____

_____

_____

_____

C. Use your partner's feedback to revise your work.

Taking It Online │ Exploring Music

A. With a partner, use the Internet to find more information about music.

ONLINE TIP
Bring music samples from the Internet only if you pay for them.

1. Choose a kind of music that you want to learn more about. Find out more about hip-hop, or any other type of music such as opera, reggae, rock, jazz, or Asian fusion. Learn about the history of the music and the influences on the musical style. Which artists are famous for this type of music? Bring a recorded sample of your musical style, if possible.

2. Use Google (www.google.com) or another major search engine to find sites with the information you want.

3. Preview the sites as you would a magazine article.

B. Complete the table with the information you find.

Music
Type of music:
Name of Website:
Website address:
When did people first start playing this music?
Which country or culture did this music come from?
What person or people were important in the beginnings of this type of music?
Does this type of music have influences from other cultures? If yes, which ones?
What are the characteristics of this type of music?
Other facts:

C. Following up. Share your facts with your classmates. Which types of music do you know? Which types are new to you?

Global Community

Answer the questions and discuss your answers with a partner.

1. What are three problems in your community, three problems in your country, and three world problems?

2. Look at the photos. What are the people doing? What problems are they helping to solve?

3. How could people solve some of the problems you thought of in question *1* above?

Text 1 | A Young Environmentalist

1 | Getting Started

A. Look at the chart about environmental problems. Add more problems. Rank them (number them in order) from most important to least important. Then write possible causes and solutions. Discuss your ideas with a partner.

Environmental problems	Rank	Possible cause(s)	Possible solution(s)
1. water pollution			
2. air pollution			
3. weather changes			
4. types of plants and animals disappearing			
5.			
6.			

B. Compare your chart with your classmates' charts. Do you agree or disagree on how to rank the problems? Do you agree or disagree on possible causes and solutions?

READING SKILL Previewing Pictures and Captions

You can sometimes **preview** a text by looking at the pictures that come with it. Pictures often have captions, or words that describe them. Pictures and captions help to show important ideas in the text.

Review the pictures and captions from *Text 2* of Chapter 4:

1. On page 61, there is a picture of someone playing a large stringed instrument. The caption is "Andrea Brooks playing the Earth Harp."

2. On page 61, there is a picture of some people playing an unusual-looking instrument. The caption is "Another of Close's instruments."

When you look at these pictures and captions *before* you read the text, you learn a few things: The text will be about musical instruments—probably new types of instruments. The text will probably also be about the people who make and play the instruments.

2 | Active Previewing

Preview the online interview below. <u>Underline</u> the important words in the title. Look at the pictures and captions. Make predictions. Then answer the following questions with a partner.

1. What is the topic of this text?

2. What kind of information will it probably have?

3 | Reading and Recalling

A. Read the text. Stop after each paragraph. Tell a partner one thing that you remember about it.

Interview with a Young Environmentalist[1]

by Yoonhee Ha, Assistant Editor, KSTR

Environmentalist Janine Licare with volunteers of Kids Saving the Rainforest

1   Janine Licare is saving the world. She and her best friend started their own non-profit organization[2], Kids Saving the Rainforest in Costa Rica (KSTR). Today, the organization has many volunteers[3] around the world. Here's our interview with Janine.

2   **YH:** Janine, when you were only nine years old, you and a friend started Kids Saving the Rainforest, KSTR. How did you become interested in the rainforest?

JL: Well, we earned some money, but we didn't know what to do with it. Then we saw something terrible: People were cutting down all the trees around us in the rainforest. That helped us decide to try to save the rainforest.

continued

---

[1] **environmentalist:** a person who works to save the natural world

[2] **non-profit organization:** an organization with the goal of doing good work—not making money

[3] **volunteers:** people who work without getting paid

continued

3   **YH:** Why do you think it's so important to save the rainforest?

    JL: The rainforest is a very important part of our earth. The trees are our lungs[4]. They help the earth breathe and stay healthy. If the trees go away, so does the future of our planet.

4   **YH:** How can our readers help you save rainforests?

    JL: They can go to the KSTR Website and learn about becoming a volunteer for the earth, for example, by buying wood from legal places and by recycling[5].

5   **YH:** How many volunteers are in your organization?

    JL: We have over 50 volunteers around the world. We also have two volunteers working with us here in Costa Rica at the KSTR office.

6   **YH:** Many of our readers do not know Costa Rica. Can you tell us what the country is like?

    JL: It's a very nice and peaceful place. The people are very kind and the rainforest is beautiful.

7   **YH:** Can you tell us what you've learned from doing this work?

    JL: We now know that we have the power to change the world and make it a better place.

8   **YH:** And what have you learned from working with people around the world?

    JL: I've learned from them that everyone is unique[6], and that we need to respect each person.

9   **YH:** Thank you for talking with us today, Janine.

    JL: You're very welcome.

---

[4] **lungs:** two organs in the chest that you use when breathing
[5] **recycling:** reusing materials such as paper, wood, metal, and glass
[6] **unique:** one of a kind; special

B. Read the text again without stopping. Tell your partner two new pieces of information that you remember.

C. Work as a class or in large groups. Try to say as many things as you can about the text.

78 | Chapter 5

4 | Understanding the Topic and the Main Idea

Write *T* for the *Topic* of *Text 1*, *G* for *Too General*, and *S* for *Too Specific*.

1. What is the topic of *Text 1*?

   a. _____ saving the rainforests in Costa Rica

   b. _____ how one person is helping to save the rainforests in Costa Rica

   c. _____ volunteering for KSTR

2. What is the main idea of *Text 1*?

   a. _____ Environmentalist Janine Licare is helping to save the rainforest.

   b. _____ The KSTR organization has 50 volunteers around the world.

   c. _____ The rainforest is a very important part of our earth.

5 | Understanding the Text

A. Answer as many questions as you can without looking at the text. Discuss your answers with a partner.

1. In which country is Janine Licare's organization, Kids Saving the Rainforest (KSTR)?

   _____

2. How old was Janine when she started the organization? _____

3. How many volunteers work for KSTR? _____

B. Check (✔) the things that Janine says in the interview. Try not to look at the text. Discuss your answers with a partner.

☐ 1. The earth cannot survive without trees.

☐ 2. People can help save the rainforest by recycling.

☐ 3. People can help save the rainforest by buying wood.

☐ 4. Costa Rica is a peaceful country.

☐ 5. Children make the best environmentalists.

☐ 6. People can save the rainforest by coming to Costa Rica.

☐ 7. It is possible to make the world a better place.

An **object pronoun** replaces a noun that is the object in a sentence. An object pronoun replaces a noun that comes *before* it, and it always matches the number (singular or plural) and the gender (*he, she, it*) of the noun that it replaces. The object pronouns are **me**, **you**, **him**, **her**, **it**, **us**, **you**, and **them**.

Read the examples.

1. Janine Licare started a non-profit organization. She started *it* when she was nine years old.

What is *it* in the second sentence? *It* is the non-profit organization in the first sentence.

2. KSTR has many volunteers. KSTR does not pay *them* for their work.

What does *them* refer to in the second sentence? It refers to the volunteers in the first sentence.

6 | Understanding Object Pronouns

Write the object that the pronoun refers to in *Text 1* on pages 77–78.

1. it (with it) (¶2) _____

2. it (make it) (¶7) _____

3. them (learned from them) (¶8) _____

7 | Discussing the Issues

Answer the questions and discuss your answers with a partner.

1. Do you know of any other people or organizations that work to save the environment? If yes, tell your partner about them.

2. Do you do anything to help save the environment? For example, do you recycle paper?

3. Janine Licare says, "We have the power to change the world and make it a better place." Do you agree? Why or why not?

Text 2 | "Genius" Grants

1 | Getting Started

A. Think about your answers to the questions in the chart. Then fill in the chart with information from three classmates.

Questions	Name _____	Name _____	Name _____
1. Should people get money for doing good things, such as solving problems in the world? Why or why not?			
2. What kind of people are good at solving world problems? That is, what professions do they usually have?			
3. Can an artist help solve world problems? Why or why not?			
4. What world problem would you like to solve?			

B. Discuss your chart with a partner. Were you surprised by any of the answers? Do most people agree or disagree that artists can help solve world problems? What world problems would your classmates like to solve?

2 | Active Previewing

Preview the magazine article on the next page. <u>Underline</u> the important words in the title. Make predictions. Then answer the following questions with a partner.

1. What is the topic of the text?

2. What is the main idea of the text?

> **REMEMBER**
> To preview, read the first sentence of each paragraph. See page 60 for more information on *previewing first sentences*.

A. Read the text. Stop after each paragraph. Tell a partner one thing that you remember about it.

The MacArthur "Genius" Grants[1]

1   Each year, the John D. and Catherine T. MacArthur Foundation gives prizes to very special people. These people are very smart and creative, so they are called "geniuses."

2   The winners receive $500, 000. The money comes with "no strings attached." For example, they can spend the money on anything they want.

3   People do not apply for the prizes. The foundation does not interview the people in order to choose the winners. Instead, the foundation organizes groups of nominators[2]. Nominators come from many different fields of study such as art, education, and science. They recommend the names of "geniuses" from their own fields. Then the foundation chooses the winners from the recommendations.

4   Here are some recent MacArthur Foundation winners:

5   **Gretchen Berland** is a doctor. She also is a filmmaker. She makes films about important problems in healthcare.

6   **James Carpenter** is a designer and an engineer. He designs buildings that use less energy and save money.

7   **Katherine Gottlieb** is CEO, or head, of a non-profit organization. Her organization is in Alaska. It gives excellent healthcare to poor Native Alaskans.

> The winners receive $500,000. The money comes with "no strings attached."

Gretchen Berland, doctor and filmmaker

continued

---

[1] **grants:** amounts of money given for projects
[2] **nominators:** people who suggest possible participants in a contest

continued

8   **David Green** helps to make health-care products for people in developing nations, poor countries such as India and Egypt. Some of his products help people to see and hear better.

9   **Aleksandar Hemon** is a writer. Hemon was born in Eastern Europe. He writes stories about ethnic conflict[3].

10   **Tommie Lindsey** teaches public speaking at a high school. Many of his students come from poor families. He helps many of his students to attend college.

11   **Reginald R. Robinson** is a pianist and composer. He works to save classical ragtime music[4]. He also writes new ragtime music.

12   **Amy Smith** is an engineer. She invents useful technologies for developing nations. One of her projects is a simple machine that cleans water.

Amy Smith, engineer

Reginald R. Robinson, pianist and composer

---

[3] **ethnic conflict:** fighting between cultural groups

[4] **ragtime music:** a kind of jazz music

B. Read the text again without stopping. Tell your partner two new pieces of information that you remember.

C. Work as a class or in large groups. Try to say as many things as you can about the text.

Paragraphs have **topics and main ideas** just like texts do. The **topic** of a paragraph is the subject of the paragraph. The **main idea** of a paragraph is the most important idea that the writer wants to express about the topic.

You state the topic of a paragraph as a phrase. You always state the main idea of a paragraph as a complete sentence. To identify the topic and main idea of a paragraph:

1. Do not choose a topic or main idea that is too general.

2. Do not choose a topic or main idea that is too specific.

Reread ¶**2** of *Text 1* on page 77:

The possible choices for the topic are:

a. cutting down the rainforest

b. why Janine Licare started KSTR

c. starting KSTR

The best topic for ¶**2** is *b*. It is not too general and it is not too specific.

The possible choices for the main idea are:

a. Licare started KSTR when she was just nine years old.

b. Licare earned some money and decided to start a non-profit organization with it.

c. Licare started KSTR after she saw that people were cutting down the rainforest.

The best main idea for ¶**2** is *c*. It is not too general and it is not too specific.

4 | Understanding Paragraph Topics and Main Ideas

For each question write *T* for the *Topic* or *MI* for *Main Idea*. Then write *G* for *Too General* and *S* for *Too Specific* for the other choices.

1. What is the topic of *Text 2*?

   a. _____ the MacArthur Foundation grants and some recent grant winners

   b. _____ how very creative people can help solve world problems

   c. _____ James Carpenter, a MacArthur Foundation "genius"

2. What is the main idea of *Text 2*?

   a. _____ The MacArthur Foundation gives prizes to "geniuses" in their fields.

   b. _____ Amy Smith is a recent MacArthur Foundation prizewinner.

   c. _____ The MacArthur Foundation is helping solve world problems.

3. What is the topic of ¶3?

    a. _____ choosing winners

    b. _____ how the MacArthur Foundation chooses winners

    c. _____ the backgrounds of the nominators

4. What is the main idea of ¶3?

    a. _____ The foundation does not interview the possible winners.

    b. _____ There is a special process for choosing MacArthur grant winners.

    c. _____ The MacArthur Foundation chooses the winners.

5 | Understanding the Text

A. Write *T* for *True* and *F* for *False* according to the information in the text. Try not to look at the text. Discuss your answers with a partner.

_____ 1. The MacArthur Foundation gives the genius grants once a year.

_____ 2. The winners receive $50,000.

_____ 3. The winners cannot do whatever they want with the prize money.

_____ 4. The winners must work for a non-profit organization.

_____ 5. Nominators suggest possible winners.

B. Work with a partner. Try not to look at the text. List as many professions as you can remember from the text.

teacher, engineer _____

_____

6 | Understanding Vocabulary in Context—Examples

Use examples from the *Text 2* on pages 82–83 to help you write a definition for each of the words and phrases.

1. "no strings attached" (¶2) _____

2. fields (¶3) _____

3. developing nations (¶8) _____

> **REMEMBER**
>
> Examples often follow phrases like *for example*, *such as*, and *like*. See page 59 for more on *examples*.

7 | Understanding Subject Pronouns

Write the subject that the pronoun refers to in *Text 2*.

1. they (they can) (¶2) _____

2. They (They recommend) (¶3) _____

3. She (She makes) (¶5) _____

4. It (It gives) (¶7) _____

8 | Discussing the Issues

Answer the questions and discuss your answers with a partner.

1. Who would you nominate for a MacArthur genius grant?

2. Imagine: You won the MacArthur genius grant. What will you do with the money?

3. Think about your favorite activity. It can be something that you love to do or something that you do very well—for example, a sport or a hobby. How could you use your favorite activity to help to solve a problem? Use your imagination.

Text 3 | Making a Difference

1 | Getting Started

Answer the questions and discuss your answers with a partner.

1. Make a list of ten famous people who work to solve problems in the world, your country, or your community. Think of people from the past and the present.

2. Make a list of ten famous people who cause problems in the world, your country, or your community. Think of people from the past and the present.

3. Now look at your lists. Who is the most influential (powerful or important) person on each list?

 GRAPHICS Understanding Tables

Tables show statistics in different ways. In Chapters 2 and 3, you previewed tables with top-row and left-hand column headings. Some tables have subheadings—headings that show categories within a table. Subheadings are sometimes in bold type or capital letters. When you preview a table, look for subheadings.

2 | Active Previewing

Preview the table on the next page. Then answer the questions. Discuss your answers with a partner.

1. What is the title of the table? _____

2. What words are in the top row? _____

_____

3. What do the subheadings say? _____

4. What is the topic of the table? _____

> **REMEMBER**
> Preview the table by looking at the title, especially the important words. Then look at the top-row headings and any subheadings. See page 26 for more information on *understanding and previewing tables.*

THE MOST INFLUENTIAL PEOPLE OF THE 20TH CENTURY

At the end of the 20th century, *TIME Magazine* took a poll[1]. It asked its readers: "Who were the most inflential people of the century?" The chart below shows some of the results. It shows some of the top people in four categories: world leaders, business leaders, scientists and thinkers, and heroes. It shows how they ranked, the percent of votes that they received, and the total number of votes that they received ("Tally").

To *TIME Magazine*, "influential people" caused great changes in the world during the 20th century.

RANK	NAME	PERCENT	TALLY
LEADERS AND REVOLUTIONARIES[2]			
1	Winston Churchill	33.84	1,364,933
2	Franklin Roosevelt	12.25	494,096
3	Nelson Mandela	0.23	9,670
4	John Kennedy	0.21	8,634
BUILDERS AND TITANS			
1	Henry Ford	18.76	591,624
2	Bill Gates	16.49	520,151
3	Howard Hughes	11.15	351,551
4	Steve Jobs	9.58	302,256
SCIENTISTS AND THINKERS			
1	Enrico Fermi	21.25	769,453
2	Jonas Salk	21.04	762,048
3	Alan Turing	8.52	308,806
4	Albert Einstein	1.49	54,262
HEROES AND ICONS			
1	Yuri Gagarin	35.48	2,068,760
2	Mother Teresa	1.72	100,365
3	Amelia Earhart	1.56	91,290
4	Elvis Presley	0.09	5,502

[1] **took a poll:** asked a group of people a question

[2] **leader:** a person who other people follow

3 | Scanning Tables

Scan the table on page 87 to find the answers to the questions. Discuss your answers with a partner.

1. What category is Bill Gates in? _____

2. How many votes did Enrico Fermi receive? _____

3. What category is Amelia Earhart in? _____

4. How many votes did Nelson Mandela receive? _____

5. Who ranks number 1 in the Leaders and Revolutionaries category? _____

6. What percentage of the votes did Albert Einstein receive? _____

7. Who got the most votes in the Builders and Titans category? _____

8. Who got the fewest votes in the Heroes and Icons category? _____

> **REMEMBER**
> Scan a table with percents and use them to answer questions quickly about comparisons. See page 44 for more information on *scanning tables*.

4 | Discussing the Issues

Answer the questions and discuss your answers with a partner.

1. How many of the people in the chart do you know about? What did they do? Why do you think they are on this list?

2. Do you agree with the results of the poll? Are there some people who should not be on this list? Who is missing from the list?

3. What categories would you add to this list? What people would you put in these categories?

Text 4 | What Motivates Altruism?

1 | Getting Started

A. Answer the questions and discuss your answers with a partner.

1. Why do some people like to help other people?

2. What are the characteristics of people who like to help others?

3. People who like to help others and do good things are called *altruists*. Are altruists born? Or do they learn to be this way?

B. Imagine: You are going to teach people to become altruists. How will you teach them? What will you teach them? Work with a partner.

2 | Active Previewing

Preview the academic text on the next page. <u>Underline</u> the important words in the title. Read the first sentence of each paragraph. Make predictions. Then answer the following questions with a partner.

1. What is the topic of this text? _____

2. What is the main idea of this text? _____

3. What kind of information might the author give? List at least three things.

_____

_____

_____

> **REMEMBER**
> To preview, look at the important words in the title, read the first sentence of each paragraph, look at pictures and captions, and then make predictions. See page 47 for more information on *making predictions*.

3 | Reading and Recalling

A. Read the text. Stop after each paragraph and tell a partner one thing that you remember about it.

A New College Course: What Motivates[1] Altruism?

1   Why do some people like to do good things such as helping others or saving the environment? They don't do these things for money. This is altruism, doing things for other people and not for oneself. Two Chico State University (California) professors wondered, "What motivates altruism?" To answer the question, they organized a college class at the university.

2   For the class, each student chose one altruist in the community. They spent four to five hours a week shadowing, or following, their altruist. They also went to class and read books and wrote papers on altruism.

3   Shadowing was an important part of the class. One student, Adam, followed a husband and wife. They work with many non-profit

Students helping at a homeless shelter

organizations in the community. Adam and the couple went shopping with elementary school children to buy holiday gifts for poor families. Adam also had dinner with the couple once a week and had many discussions with them about helping others. Two other students, Nicki and Ben, shadowed the director of a homeless shelter. The students served food to homeless people and they helped the director raise money[2] for the shelter.

4   The students learned many things. Adam said, "In school, we think too much about our careers. This class helped us remember that there are other important things in life. I also learned that I can help others as a career." Another student said, "Altruists are not necessarily special people. They are just ordinary people who do special things." The students also learned about the motivations for altruism. One altruist told a student: "I work for the community because the community helped me in the past." Another said: "I get great satisfaction[3] because I know that I am helping others. Recognition[4] for my work is not important."

5   The altruists also learned things from the students. The students' questions made them think.

A class on altruism

_____
[1] **motivates:** makes someone want to do something
[2] **raise money:** get money
[3] **satisfaction:** a good feeling
[4] **recognition:** appreciation; credit

continued

continued

They learned more about themselves and their motivations. This helped the altruists to become even better at their work.

6   The class on altruism was not easy for the students. They spent many hours with their altruists. They also read 250 pages every week. They read the works of great thinkers and philoso-phers, people such as Martin Luther King, Jr. and Emmanuel Kant, who think and write about the meaning of life. They wrote many papers, kept a journal, and took exams. Was it a useful class? As Adam said: "The class was difficult, but it was worth it[5]. I learned a lot. This experience will stay with me for the rest of my life."

---

[5] **it was worth it:** it had value; it was a good thing

B. Read the text again without stopping. Tell your partner two new pieces of information that you remember.

C. Work as a class or in large groups. Try to name as many things as you can about the text.

4 | Understanding the Topic and the Main Idea

Answer the questions or write *T* for the *Topic*, *MI* for *Main Idea*, *G* for *Too General*, and *S* for *Too Specific*.

1. What is the topic of *Text 4*? _____

2. What is the main idea of *Text 4*?

   a. _____ Students are taking a new college course.

   b. _____ Students are studying other people in a new college course.

   c. _____ Students are learning about altruism in a new college course.

3. Are your answers for the topic and the main idea the same as the ones you chose when you previewed the text? Explain. _____

4. What is the topic of ¶4?

   a. _____ what the students learned about altruism

   b. _____ what motivates altruism

   c. _____ what the students learned

5. What is the main idea of ¶4?

   a. _____ Altruists do not usually care about recognition for their work.

   b. _____ The students learned many things about altruists and altruism.

   c. _____ The students learned many things.

5 | Understanding the Text

A. Write *T* for *True* and *F* for *False* according to the information in the text. Try not to look at the text. Discuss your answers with a partner.

_____ 1. Students in the class worked with altruists in the community.

_____ 2. Students did not have to read books or write papers for the class.

_____ 3. The students learned why altruists do good things.

_____ 4. The altruists did not learn very much from the students.

_____ 5. One student learned that altruism could be a career.

B. Check (✔) the characteristics of the altruists in the text. Discuss your answers with a partner.

☐ 1. They think that getting paid for their work is important.

☐ 2. They get satisfaction from helping others.

☐ 3. They do not need recognition.

☐ 4. They are special people who do ordinary things.

☐ 5. They became better at their work because of the students.

READING SKILL Understanding Supporting Details

A **supporting detail** supports a main idea. That means it proves or explains a main idea. Writers use details to develop their ideas. Supporting details can be facts, opinions, statistics, and examples.

Reread ¶4 of *Text 4* on page 89.

The main idea is: The students learned many things about altruists and altruism.

Some of the supporting details are:

1. Adam learned that there are other things in life besides a career.

2. Another student learned that altruists are ordinary people who do special things.

3. One student learned that altruists do what they do because helping others gives them satisfaction.

These details show examples of the things the students learned about altruism and altruists.

6 | Understanding Supporting Details

Answer the questions about *Text 4*. Check (✔) the supporting details. Discuss your answers with a partner.

1. What is the main idea of ¶3? _____

2. What are the two supporting details for the main idea of ¶3?

   ☐ a. Poor families can't afford to buy holiday presents.

   ☐ b. Nicki and Ben helped to raise money for a homeless shelter.

   ☐ c. Adam had many discussions with his altruists.

3. What is the main idea of ¶6? _____

4. What are the two supporting details for the main idea of ¶6?

   ☐ a. The students spent many hours with their altruists.

   ☐ b. Philosophers are people who think and write about the meaning of life.

   ☐ c. The students read 250 pages a week.

7 | Understanding Vocabulary in Context—Synonyms, Definitions, and Examples

Read the following sentences from *Text 4*. Circle the part of speech for the underlined words. Then write their meanings on the lines. Look for synonyms, definitions, and examples.

1. This is <u>altruism</u>, doing things for other people and not for oneself.

   ☐ a. noun   ☐ b. verb   ☐ c. adjective

   _____

2. They spent four to five hours a week <u>shadowing</u>, or following, their altruist.

   ☐ a. noun   ☐ b. verb   ☐ c. adjective

   _____

3. They read the works of great thinkers and <u>philosophers</u>, people such as Martin Luther King, Jr. and Emmanuel Kant, who think and write about the meaning of life.

   ☐ a. noun   ☐ b. verb   ☐ c. adjective

   _____

8 | Discussing the Issues

Answer the questions and discuss your answers with a partner.

1. Would you like to take a class on altruism? Why or why not?

2. Would you like to help others as a career? Why or why not?

3. What are some things you do to help solve problems in the world, in your country, or in your community? What would you like to do in the future?

Putting It On Paper

A. Write a paragraph on one of these topics.

1. What is the most important problem to solve in the world today? Why is it the most important problem?

2. Can a person learn to be an altruist? Explain your answer.

Steps for your paragraph

   a. State the main idea of your paragraph in the first sentence. This is your topic sentence.

   b. Include in your paragraph three supporting details that explain your idea. Use facts, opinions, statistics, and/or examples.

   c. Try to use words and expressions from this chapter.

B. Exchange paragraphs with a partner. Read your partner's paragraph. Answer the questions in the checklist. Give feedback to your partner.

✔ CHECKLIST
1. Is there a clear main idea?
2. Are there enough supporting details? What types of supporting details are they?
3. Do all the supporting details connect to the main idea?
4. Are there words and expressions from this chapter?
5. Write additional comments below.

_____

_____

_____

_____

_____

_____

_____

_____

_____

C. Use your partner's feedback to revise your work.

Taking It Online | Problem Solving

A. With a partner, use the Internet to find more information about organizations or people who work to solve problems.

ONLINE TIP

Combine key words:
saving the rainforest + organizations
weather changes + organizations
pollution + organizations

1. Choose a problem that interests you. Then find organizations that are working on the problem. Find out what they are doing. Find out how other people can help. For example, if you are interested in saving the rainforest, look for organizations or groups of people that are working on this.

2. Use Google (www.google.com) or another major search engine to find sites with the information you want.

3. Preview the sites as you would a magazine article.

B. Complete the table with the information you find.

Problem
The problem:
Name of Website/Name of organization:
Website address:
What kind of information does this organization have on its website?
What projects is this organization involved in?
What can people do to help solve the problem?
What can people do to help the organization?
Other facts:

C. Following up. Share your facts with your classmates. Which organizations would you like to help? Why?

Business Etiquette

Answer the questions and discuss your answers with a partner.

1. Are the rules for polite social behavior—ways to act with other people—different in different countries or cultures? If yes, give an example.

2. Look at the photos. What are the people doing? Compare the people: How is their behavior similar? How is it different?

3. What are some of the rules for polite business behavior—ways to act with people in business situations—that might be different in different countries or cultures?

Text 1 | Etiquette Intelligence

1 | Getting Started

A. Answer the questions and discuss your answers with a partner.

1. Describe polite behavior in the following social situations. Give your opinion.

   a. introducing people to each other

   b. using cell phones

   c. eating dinner or lunch in a restaurant

   d. giving gifts

2. Would your descriptions in number *1* be different if these were business situations? Explain.

   _____

   _____

   _____

3. Is polite business behavior in North American culture (in the United States and Canada) the same as or different from polite business behavior in other cultures? Give examples. If you aren't sure, guess.

   _____

   _____

   _____

2 | Active Previewing

Preview the online quiz below. <u>Underline</u> the important words in the title. Make predictions. Then answer the following questions with a partner.

1. What is the topic of this quiz?
2. What kind of information will it have?

3 | Reading and Recalling

Read the text. Stop after each paragraph and circle your answer. Do not read the correct answers yet.

What Is Your Business "EQ", Your Etiquette Intelligence?

What is polite behavior in North American business situations? Test your business EQ, your etiquette[1] intelligence. Choose the best answer for each situation.

1. In a business situation,

    a. only men should stand up for introductions and to shake hands.

    b. only women should stand up for introductions and to shake hands.

    c. it is not necessary for men or women to stand up for introductions or to shake hands.

    d. both men and women should stand up for introductions and to shake hands.

2. In a business situation at a restaurant, a man should

    a. pull a chair out for a woman.

    b. stand when a woman leaves the table.

    c. pay for a woman's meal.

    d. All of the above.

    e. None of the above.

3. The best way to meet people at a business event is to

    a. stay with the people you know very well and forget about everyone else.

    b. stay with the people you know and wait for them to introduce you to other people.

    c. look confident[2], stand in the center of the room, and wait for someone to come to you.

    d. introduce yourself to people.

4. At work, an angry customer calls to complain[3]. You

    a. put the person on hold[4] and do something else.

    b. tell the caller that he or she has the wrong number and hang up.

    c. stay calm, listen to the caller's complaint, and try to help him or her.

    d. give the customer to a coworker.

5. You have to introduce two people. You can't remember one person's name. You say

    a. "Do you know each other?"

    b. "I can't remember your name. Why don't you introduce yourselves?"

continued

---

[1] **etiquette:** polite behavior; good manners

[2] **confident:** sure of yourself

[3] **complain/complaint:** tell about a problem/a problem

[4] **put the person on hold:** tell the person to wait on the phone while you do something else

[5] **embarrass:** make someone feel ashamed or uncomfortable

continued

    c. nothing. You do not want to embarrass⁵ yourself or others.

    d. "I'm sorry. Please tell me your name again."

6. You have to introduce a visitor to your company president. You

    a. introduce the person that you know well to the person that you do not know as well.

    b. introduce the visitor to the president.

    c. introduce the president to the visitor.

    d. do not do anything. It is their responsibility to introduce themselves to each other.

7. When you thank someone for a business gift, you

    a. send an e-mail.

    b. send a handwritten note.

    c. call him or her on the phone as soon as possible.

    d. just say "thank you" when you get the gift.

8. At a business dinner in a restaurant, your cell phone rings. You

    a. answer your phone but talk only for a short time.

    b. ignore it and pretend that someone else's phone is ringing.

    c. apologize and turn the phone off.

    d. apologize, leave the table, and answer the phone in another part of the restaurant.

Correct Answers

In North American business culture, the following answers are correct:

1.d; 2.e; 3.d; 4.c; 5.d; 6.c; 7.b; 8.c

B. Read the text again without stopping. This time, read the correct answers. Tell your partner two new pieces of information that you remember.

C. Work as a class or in large groups. Try to say as many things as you can about the text.

4 | Understanding the Topic and the Main Idea

Answer the questions. Write *T* for the *Topic*, *MI* for *Main Idea*, *G* for *Too General*, and *S* for *Too Specific*.

1. What is the topic of *Text 1*?

    a. _____ cell phone etiquette

    b. _____ business etiquette in North America

    c. _____ business etiquette

2. What is the main idea of *Text 1*?

    a. _____ There are certain rules for correct business etiquette in North America.

    b. _____ There are certain rules for behavior in social situations in North America.

    c. _____ There are certain rules for introducing business people in North America.

5 | Understanding the Text

A. Write *T* for *True* and *F* for *False* according to the information in the text. Try not to look at the text. Discuss your answers with a partner.

_____ **1.** A man should pull out a woman's chair at a business dinner.

_____ **2.** You should introduce yourself at a business event.

_____ **3.** If you cannot remember someone's name, it's OK to say, "I can't remember your name."

_____ **4.** It's OK to send an e-mail thank you note for a business gift.

_____ **5.** It's OK to talk on a cell phone at a business dinner if you do not talk too long.

B. Take the quiz again. Try not to look at the answers. Did you get all correct answers this time?

6 | Understanding Object Pronouns

> **REMEMBER**
>
> An object pronoun replaces a noun that is the object in a sentence. See page 80 for more on *understanding object pronouns*.

Write the object that the pronoun refers to in *Text 1* on pages 96–98.

1. them (wait for them) (**Q3**) _____

2. him or her (help him or her) (**Q4**) _____

3. him or her (call him or her) (**Q7**) _____

4. it (ignore it) (**Q8**) _____

7 | Discussing the Issues

Answer the questions and discuss your answers with a partner.

1. Did any of the rules for North American business etiquette surprise you? If yes, which ones?

2. How do the rules for North American business etiquette differ from business etiquette rules in another country or culture that you know?

3. Describe your experiences with business etiquette in different countries or cultures.

Text 2 | Polite Business Behavior

1 | Getting Started

A. Think about your answers to the questions in the chart. Then fill in the chart with information from three classmates.

Questions	Name _____	Name _____	Name _____
1. What do you do when you meet someone for the first time? What do you say? Do you use any body language such as shaking hands?			
2. In what situations would you kiss another person?			
3. In what situations would you hug another person?			
4. During a conversation, would you touch the other person's arm, shoulder, or back?			

B. Compare your chart with a partner's chart. Discuss the similarities and differences.

2 | Active Previewing

Preview the magazine article on the next page. Make predictions. Then answer the following questions with a partner.

1. What is the topic of the text?
2. What is the main idea of the text?

3 | Reading and Recalling

A. Read the text. Stop after each paragraph. Tell a partner one thing that you remember about it.

> **REMEMBER**
>
> To preview, look at the important words in the title. Read the first sentence of each paragraph. Look at pictures and captions. Then make predictions. See page 47 for more information on *making predictions*.

Polite Behavior in Four Countries

1   The first meeting with a new person, especially in business, can be very important. When you are in another country, do you know how to greet someone? How important is eye contact, looking into the other person's eyes while you speak? How important is personal distance, the space between you and the other person? Here are some tips[1] on polite behavior in four countries.

2 Australia

- People shake hands when greeting each other.
- It is the custom to shake hands at the beginning and end of a meeting.
- It is polite for visitors to introduce themselves in social situations.
- When you speak to an Australian, keep an arm's length distance[2] from the person. Maintaining[3] personal distance is important in this culture.
- Make eye contact with an Australian when conversing[4].

3 Brazil

- Brazilians usually stand very close to each other.
- Brazilians usually greet each other with long handshakes and eye contact; close friends often hug.
- Hugging and backslapping are common among Brazilians, but they usually do not do this with foreigners.
- Brazilians often touch each other's arms, hands, or shoulders during a conversation.

4 South Korea

- In South Korea, don't introduce yourself; wait for someone to introduce you to other people.
- South Korean men often greet each other with a slight bow and sometimes also with a handshake.
- Bow at the beginning and end of a meeting.
- Some Koreans believe that it's impolite to maintain eye contact with a person who has high status[5].
- In formal situations, Koreans usually do not touch each other's arms or backs during conversations. Touching is impolite with older people, people of the opposite sex, or people who are not good friends or family.

5 Turkey

- When you meet someone in Turkey, shake hands firmly.
- Friends and family often greet each other with either one or two kisses on the cheek.
- When you enter a room, if someone does not greet you first, greet the oldest person or the person with the highest status first. In social situations, greet the person closest to you, then move around the room or table counter-clockwise.

Personal distance in Australia

Hugging in Brazil

Bowing in South Korea

Greeting in Turkey

---

[1] **tips:** suggestions

[2] **keep an arm's length distance:** stand as far away as the length of an arm

[3] **Maintaining:** keeping

[4] **conversing:** talking; having a conversation

[5] **status:** position; place in a company or in a social group

B. Read the text again without stopping. Tell your partner two new pieces of information that you remember.

C. Work as a class or in large groups. Try to say as many things as you can about the text.

4 | Understanding the Topic and the Main Idea

Answer the questions. Write *T* for the *Topic*, *MI* for *Main Idea*, *G* for *Too General*, and *S* for *Too Specific*.

1. What is the topic of *Text 2*?

   a. _____ polite business behavior in four cultures

   b. _____ polite business behavior

   c. _____ how to greet people in Australia

2. What is the main idea of *Text 2*?

   a. _____ It's important to know how to greet people in business situations.

   b. _____ It's impolite to introduce yourself in some countries.

   c. _____ Polite business behavior is different in different cultures.

3. What is the topic of ¶2?

   a. _____ shaking hands in Australia

   b. _____ polite business behavior in Australia

   c. _____ polite behavior in Australia

4. What is the main idea of ¶2?

   a. _____ Australians have particular rules for greeting and conversing in business situations.

   b. _____ Australian rules for greeting and conversing are different from other culture's rules.

   c. _____ It's important to make eye contact when you are conversing with an Australian.

5 | Understanding the Text

A. Fill in the chart with behavior rules from the four cultures discussed in *Text 2*. Try not to look at the text. Discuss your answers with a partner. Note: Not every culture has rules for every behavior.

Cultures	Greetings	Maintaining personal distance	Introductions	Touching
1. Australian				
2. Brazilian				
3. South Korean				
4. Turkish				

B. Use the Venn diagram to compare business behavior in two cultures. Choose two cultures from *Text 2* or two other cultures that you know. Write the similarities and differences.

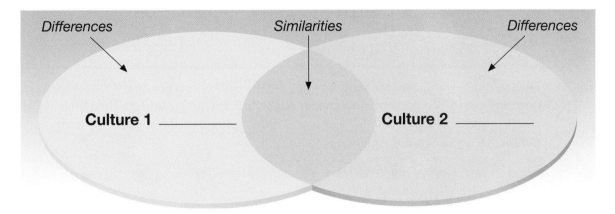

Differences   *Similarities*   *Differences*

Culture 1 _____   **Culture 2** _____

6 | Understanding Vocabulary in Context—Definitions

Use context to help you guess the meaning of each expression from *Text 2*.

1. eye contact (¶1) _____

2. personal distance (¶1) _____

7 | Discussing the Issues

Answer the questions and discuss your answers with a partner.

1. Which cultures in *Text 2* have behavior rules that involve gender (males and females)? Which cultures have rules that involve status? What other cultures might have rules like these? Give examples.

2. Do you have experience with any of the cultures in *Text 2*? If yes, do you agree or disagree with the tips?

3. How might the information in *Text 2* be useful? Give examples.

Text 3 | Too Close or Too Far?

1 | Getting Started

Discuss your answers with a partner.

1. How far away do you stand from another person in the following situations?

   a. talking with a family member   c. talking with someone in a business situation

   b. talking with a friend   d. talking with a stranger

2. Stand up with your partner. Show the distances between you for each situation in number *1*. If possible, measure the distances.

3. For each situation in number *1*, discuss what might happen if you stand too close or too far away from the person.

GRAPHICS Previewing Diagrams

Diagrams show information visually, with pictures or other types of graphics such as lines and circles. To preview diagrams, read the title and any subtitles. Then look at the whole diagram at once. Look for words and numbers. Think about what the words and numbers tell you about the pictures

2 | Active Previewing

Preview the diagram below. Then answer the questions. Discuss your answers with a partner.

1. What is the title of the diagram? _____

2. Are there any subtitles? _____

3. What kind of pictures are in the diagram? What do they show? What other types of graphics are there? What do they show?

_____

_____

4. What words are in the diagram? What do they tell you?

_____

_____

5. What do the numbers in the diagram tell you? _____

6. What is the topic of the diagram? _____

Personal Distance in Different Cultures

Edward Hall, an anthropologist[1], studied the differences in personal distance in cultures around the world. He learned this: North Americans maintain about 4 feet between them during business conversations. Some cultures – for example, Mediterranean – stand closer during a conversation. Some cultures – for example, some Asian cultures – stand farther apart. The following diagram shows the distance for communicating with business people in six cultures.

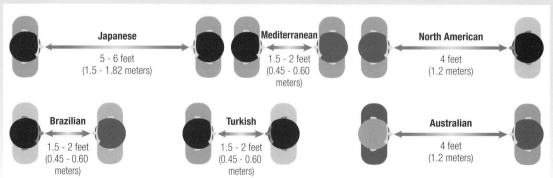

Japanese
5 - 6 feet
(1.5 - 1.82 meters)

Mediterranean
1.5 - 2 feet
(0.45 - 0.60 meters)

North American
4 feet
(1.2 meters)

Brazilian
1.5 - 2 feet
(0.45 - 0.60 meters)

Turkish
1.5 - 2 feet
(0.45 - 0.60 meters)

Australian
4 feet
(1.2 meters)

Note: *Distances are approximate.*[2]

GRAPHICS Scanning Diagrams

When you **scan diagrams**, use the pictures and other graphics to find answers quickly. The visual information in pictures and graphics can sometimes give you answers faster than words can.

3 | Scanning Diagrams

Scan the diagram on page 104 to find the answers to the questions. Discuss your answers with a partner.

1. How far apart do people in Mediterranean cultures stand in a business conversation? Give your answer in feet and in meters. _____

2. How far apart do people in Turkish culture stand in a business conversation? Give your answer in feet and in meters. _____

3. Which cultures have similar amounts of personal distance? _____

4. According to the diagram, which cultures are the most different? _____

5. Which culture has the greatest amount of personal distance? _____

6. Which cultures have the least amount of personal distance? _____

4 | Discussing the Issues

Answer the questions and discuss your answers with a partner.

1. Do you have experience with any of the cultures in the diagram? If yes, do you agree or disagree with the information?

2. How might the information in the diagram be useful? Give examples.

3. Choose one of the situations in *Getting Started*, number *1*, page 103. Make diagrams to show the differences in personal distance among the students in class. If most people's answers are the same, show the differences in personal distance for each of the situations in number *1*.

Text 4 | Interviewing for a Job

1 | Getting Started

A. Answer the questions and discuss your answers with a partner.

1. How do you get a job in your country? How might you get a job in a different country? Are there any differences?

2. How do you prepare for a job interview in your country? How might you prepare for a job interview in another country? Are there any differences?

3. How do you behave in a job interview in your country? How might you behave in a job interview in another country? Are there any differences?

B. Make a list of things that are important in a job interview (for example, appearance and work experience). Then rank the items in your list. Discuss your list with a partner.

 READING SKILL Skimming

Skimming is moving your eyes over a text as you read quickly. You skim when you want to get a general idea about the information in the text but do not need to know all of the details.

Skimming is a good way to preview a text. It also helps you save time. For example, you skim when you want to see if the full text is something you want to read or if it will have the information you need.

To skim:

1. Read the title and any subtitles.

2. Read one or two paragraphs at the beginning.

3. Read the first and/or last sentence of the other paragraphs.

4. Look quickly at the other paragraphs. Read only a few words here and there. Notice names, places, dates and numbers, and words in bold or italic print.

5. Read the last paragraph.

2 | Skimming

Skim the academic text on the next page in three minutes or less. Then answer the following questions with a partner.

1. Is this article useful for someone who is going to have a job interview in another country?

_____

2. What is the topic of this text? _____

3. What is the main idea of this text? _____

4. What kind of information will the author probably give? Name at least three things.

_____

A. Read the text. Stop after each paragraph. Tell a partner one thing that you remember about it.

Job Interviewing Across Cultures

1   Job interviews can be very stressful[1]. They are stressful in your own country or culture. However, in another country or culture, a job interview can be especially difficult. In your own country or culture, you usually know what to expect, but how do you prepare for a job interview in another country?

2   There are two important questions to ask before you have a job interview in another country or culture: First, what does the interviewer expect? Second, how do job interviews in this country differ from job interviews in your country?

3   The key to job interview success is simple: Be prepared. However, preparation is difficult if you are not familiar with a culture or country. To prepare, you may want to read books on the culture of the country. You can also ask local people to tell you about job interviews in their country.

4   Before you have your interview, try to find out about the following:

5   • **Dress:** What do people in this country usually wear to a job interview? Do different types of companies have different ideas about how to dress? For example, in Country X, you should wear business clothes to an interview for a job at a bank. However, you can wear informal clothes to an interview for a job at a department store.

6   • **Your role in the interview:** In some cultures, you should "sell" yourself during the interview. For example, you should talk a lot about your credentials and your skills[2]. In other cultures, you should not talk as much. Instead, you should talk less and wait for the interviewer to ask you questions.

An interview at a bank

7   • **Correct etiquette:** In some cultures, your behavior is more important than your credentials. In this case, the interviewer might be evaluating[3] your politeness and etiquette. In other cultures, experience and credentials are more important than etiquette.

8   • **The pace[4] of the interview:** In some cultures, the interview may move slowly. The interviewer might ask you many questions. These questions may seem indirect—that is, less clear. In other cultures, the interview may move quickly. The interviewer might ask questions directly and quickly.

9   • **Relationships:** In some cultures, personal relationships are important. For example, a friend or acquaintance might introduce you to an interviewer or to a company. This might help you to get the job. In other cultures, your experience and credentials are more important than who you know.

10 • **The value of educational credentials as opposed to experience:** In some cultures, diplomas, certificates, and written references[5] are important. In other cultures, experience is more important than credentials and diplomas.

continued

---

[1] **stressful:** causing nervousness or anxiety

[2] **your skills:** your abilities; things that you know how to do

[3] **evaluating:** judging; making decisions about

[4] **pace:** speed; how fast or how slow

[5] **references:** what people say about you, especially about your work

continued

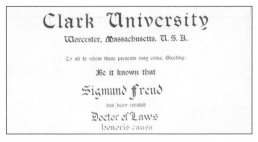

Credentials

Company Website

11   Finally, you should do research on the company. Check websites for background information on the company. Try to find the answers to questions such as these: Where does the company do business? Who are the important people in the company? What is the company proud of? If you're well prepared, you'll do well in any job interview, either at home or in another country.

B. Read the text again without stopping. Tell your partner two new pieces of information that you remember.

C. Work as a class or in large groups. Try to name as many things as you can about the text.

4 | Understanding the Topic, Main Idea, and Supporting Details

A. Answer the questions or write *T* for the *Topic*, *MI* for *Main Idea*, *G* for *Too General*, and *S* for *Too Specific*.

1. What is the topic of *Text 4*? _____

2. What is the main idea of *Text 4*?

   a. _____ In some cultures, your relationships are more important than your credentials.

   b. _____ There are certain things that you can do to prepare for a job interview.

   c. _____ How to behave in a job interview differs from culture to culture.

3. Are your answers for the topic and the main idea the same as the ones you chose when you previewed the text? Explain. _____

4. What is the topic of ¶**11**?

   a. _____ doing research on companies before the job interview

   b. _____ using websites to do research

   c. _____ finding out who the important people in a company are

5. What is the main idea of ¶**11**?

   a. _____ It's a good idea to check the website of a company before you have a job interview.

   b. _____ It's a good idea to find out who the important people in the company are before an interview.

   c. _____ It's a good idea to do research on companies.

B. Check (✔) the two supporting details. Discuss your answers with a partner.

1. What are the two supporting details for the main idea of ¶3?

    ☐ a. You can read books about the culture before a job interview.

    ☐ b. There are books about different countries' cultures.

    ☐ c. You can talk to local people about job interviews in their country.

2. What are the two supporting details for the main idea of ¶7?

    ☐ a. In some countries, interviews go slowly.

    ☐ b. In some cultures, the interviewer asks a lot of questions.

    ☐ c. In some cultures, the interviewer asks too many questions.

5 | Understanding the Text

A. Write *T* for *True* and *F* for *False* according to the information in the text. Try not to look at the text. Discuss your answers with a partner.

_____ 1. There are cultural differences in how much you should talk during a job interview.

_____ 2. People wear business clothes to an interview at a bank in all countries.

_____ 3. Information about your college or about your studies are examples of credentials.

_____ 4. In some cultures, your relationships with other people can help you get a job.

_____ 5. It is not necessary to do research on a company before an interview.

B. Fill in the chart with things to consider at a job interview. They can be examples from the text or your own examples. Try not to look at the text. Work with a partner.

Job interviews	
Things to consider	**Examples**
1. dress	
2. talking during the interview	
3. credentials	
4. relationships	*In my culture, you often get a job because you know someone important in the company.*
5. experience	
6. politeness	

Collocations are groups of words. They often appear together. Sometimes you can understand collocations from the context of the sentence. Sometimes you will need to look them up in a dictionary that contains collocations (not all dictionaries include them).

Read the following sentence.

How importat is *eye contact,* looking into the other person's eyes while you speak?

Eye contact is a collocation. What does it mean? The second half of the sentence tells you that *eye contact* means *looking into the other person's eyes while you speak.*

Memorize collocations as groups of words. Notice their part of speech and how they fit into sentences. Look for context clues to help you understand them.

6 | Understanding Vocabulary in Context—Collocations

Select the best meaning for each collocation according to *Text 4*.

1. sell yourself (¶6)

   a. listen quietly   b. talk about money   c. talk about yourself

2. as opposed to (¶10)

   a. against   b. just like   c. together with

3. do research (¶11)

   a. work for   b. learn about   c. ignore

4. do business (¶11)

   a. have its main office   b. want to do its work   c. do its work

7 | Discussing the Issues

Answer the questions and discuss your answers with a partner.

1. What is your ideal job—the perfect job for you? In what kind of company or organization would you like to do this job?

2. Would you like to work in a different country? Why or why not?

3. Imagine: You have moved to another country and you're working at your ideal job there. What parts of your job are the same as a similar job at home? What parts are different?

Putting It On Paper

A. Write a paragraph on one of these topics.

1. Would you like to get a job in another country? Why or why not?

2. Why is it important to know the rules of business behavior in different countries?

Steps for your paragraph

a. State the main idea of your paragraph in the first sentence. This is your topic sentence.

b. Include in your paragraph three supporting details that explain your idea. Use facts, opinions, statistics, and/or examples.

c. Try to use words and expressions you learned in this chapter.

B. Exchange paragraphs with a partner. Read your partner's paragraph. Answer the questions in the checklist. Give feedback to your partner.

✔ CHECKLIST
1. Is there a clear main idea?
2. Are there enough supporting details? What types of supporting details are they?
3. Do all the supporting details connect to the main idea?
4. Are there words and expressions from this chapter?
5. Write additional comments below.

_____

_____

_____

_____

_____

_____

_____

_____

_____

C. Use your partner's feedback to revise your work.

Taking It Online | Exploring Companies

A. With a partner, use the Internet to find information about companies.

1. Think about a company that interests you. Look at the company's home page to find out what kind of information the company website has. What kind of background information can you get about the company?

2. Use Google (www.google.com) or another major search engine to find sites with the information you want.

3. Preview the sites the same way you would preview a magazine article.

B. Complete the table with the information you find.

> **ONLINE TIP**
>
> Look at the navigation bar on the home page of a website. This will tell you the categories of information on that website. The navigation bar is usually at the top or on the left-hand side of the page.

Company
Company name:
Name of Website:
Website address:
What kind of company is this? What do they do?
What kind of information does this organization have on its website?
Can you find out who the important people in the company are? If yes, list some of them.
Where does the company do business? Do employees work in many countries or just their home country?
Does the company list available jobs? If yes, give some examples.
Other facts:

C. Following up. Share your facts with your classmates. Explain your choices. How many companies do business in other countries? Which companies would you like to work for?

Fashion Philosophy

Answer the questions and discuss your answers with a partner.

1. Do you think a lot about your clothes? Why or why not?

2. Look at the photos. What are the people wearing? Use as many descriptive words as you can, for example, words for styles, sizes, and shapes.

3. What are you wearing today? Why are you wearing it?

Text 1 | A Thai Fashion Designer

1 | Getting Started

A. Answer the questions and discuss your answers with a partner.

1. Name some fashion designers. Where are they from? What do they design?

2. What kind of person is a fashion designer? What are the characteristics of a fashion designer? What skills do they have?

3. Would you like to be a fashion designer? Why or why not?

B. Imagine: You are going to interview a fashion designer. What questions will you ask? Discuss your questions with a partner.

2 | Active Previewing

Preview the online interview below. <u>Underline</u> the important words in the title. Read the first sentence of each paragraph. Make predictions. Then answer the following questions with a partner.

1. What is the topic of this text?

2. What kind of information will it have?

> **REMEMBER**
> Look at the pictures and captions to make predictions. See page 76 for more information on previewing pictures and captions.

3 | Reading and Recalling

A. Read the text. Stop after each paragraph. Tell a partner one thing that you remember about it.

Style Interview: Fashion Designer Khun Lee

by Paul Vargas

Thai fashion designer Khun Lee

1   Khun Lee is a Thai fashion designer. Her fashions are popular around the world. Fashion writer Paul Vargas met her and asked her a few questions.

2   **PV:** Today, I am talking with the Thai fashion designer Khun Lee. Lee is the designer for Senada Theory fashions. Khun, how do you describe your style?

KL: Well, Paul, I like to describe my fashion this way: Exciting and hip[1].

continued

---

[1] **hip:** modern and youthful

continued

3   **PV:** You mix traditional styles with modern styles, right?

     KL: Right. We combine traditional, ethnic Thai styles with modern, cutting-edge, European styles. We also use vintage styles, for example, European and Thai styles from the past.

4   **PV:** Can you give me an example?

     KL: Sure. We might use a traditional Thai ceramics design in a fabric pattern. Or antique[2] Thai cloth in a dress.

5   **PV:** Tell me more about how you work.

     KL: We use batik, embroidery, and block printing. These are traditional Thai textile[3] designs. We also use a very special Thai silk.

6   **PV:** Now, who are your customers?

     KL: Our customers are usually women between the ages of 20 and 40. They like fashion, and they are creative and original.

Block printing

7   **PV:** Tell me a little about your background.

     KL: Well, my background wasn't originally in fashion. My academic background[4] is in biochemical science. But my hobby was always clothing design.

8   **PV:** How did you get started?

     KL: I started sewing wedding dresses. At the same time, I started collecting vintage clothing from the United States, France, and Thailand.

9   **PV:** When did you open your first store?

     KL: I opened my first Senada Theory store in the Siam Centre in 2002. We now have a second store in Gaysorn.

10   **PV:** I know you're a very busy person. What else do you do?

     KL: Yes, I'm also the secretary of the Bangkok Fashion Society. It's an organization of designers. We work to promote Thai fashion, to advertise Thai fashion around the world.

Some Senada Theory fashions

11   **PV:** Can people buy your fashions outside of Thailand?

     KL: Sure. You can find my fashions in top design stores from London to Milan, and from Tokyo to Singapore.

---

[2] **antique:** very old

[3] **textile:** cloth

[4] **academic background:** educational background; studies

B. Read the text again without stopping. Tell your partner two new pieces of information that you remember.

C. Work as a class or in large groups. Try to say as many things as you can about the text.

4 | Understanding the Topic and the Main Idea

Answer the questions. Write *T* for the *Topic*, *MI* for *Main Idea*, *G* for *Too General*, and *S* for *Too Specific*.

1. What is the topic of *Text 1*?

   a. _____ Thai fashion designers

   b. _____ Khun Lee, a Thai fashion designer

   c. _____ Senada Theory fashions

2. What is the main idea of *Text 1*?

   a. _____ Thai designer Khun Lee designs modern styles with traditional influences.

   b. _____ All Thai fashion designers design modern styles with traditional influences.

   c. _____ Thai designer Khun Lee designs modern styles in Thai silk.

5 | Understanding the Text

A. Answer as many questions as you can without looking at *Text 1*. Discuss your answers with a partner.

1. Khun Lee's fashions are

   a. modern.

   b. traditional.

   c. a mix of modern and traditional.

2. Khun Lee's customers are

   a. men and women between the ages of 20 and 40.

   b. women from the ages of 20 to 30.

   c. women from the ages of 20 to 40.

3. Khun Lee's academic background was originally in

   a. fashion design.

   b. biochemistry.

   c. sewing.

4. Khun Lee's hobby was

    a. designing clothes.

    b. studying biochemistry.

    c. sewing wedding dresses.

5. Khun Lee also works for an organization that

    a. promotes Thailand.

    b. promotes Thai fashion.

    c. promotes Thai products.

B. Check (✔) the things that Khun Lee did (or does). Try not to look at the text. Discuss your answers with a partner.

   ☐ **1.** works as the secretary of the Bangkok Fashion Society

   ☐ **2.** studied in France

   ☐ **3.** collected vintage clothing from the United States, France, and Thailand

   ☐ **4.** sewed vintage clothing in the United States

   ☐ **5.** opened the Senada Theory store

   ☐ **6.** studied biochemistry

   ☐ **7.** designed batik textiles

   ☐ **8.** sewed wedding dresses

6 | Understanding Vocabulary in Context—Synonyms, Definitions, and Examples

Read the following sentences from *Text 1*. Circle the part of speech for the underlined words. Then write their meanings on the lines. Look for synonyms, definitions, and examples.

1. We combine traditional, ethnic Thai styles with modern, <u>cutting-edge</u>, European styles.

   ☐ a. noun   ☐ b. verb   ☐ c. adjective

_____

2. We also use <u>vintage</u> styles, for example, European and Thai styles from the past.

   ☐ a. noun   ☐ b. verb   ☐ c. adjective

_____

3. They like fashion, and they are creative and <u>original</u>.

   ☐ a. noun   ☐ b. verb   ☐ c. adjective

_____

7 | Discussing the Issues

Answer the questions and discuss your answers with a partner.

1. Do you like clothes that are a mixture of modern and traditional styles? Why or why not?

2. How do clothing types differ in different cultures? Give examples.

3. How do fashion styles differ in different cultures? Give examples.

Text 2 | The 80s Look

1 | Getting Started

A. Answer the questions and discuss your answers with a partner.

1. What are some popular clothing styles today? Find some examples in your class.

2. Are your parents' clothes different from your clothes? If yes, how?

B. Make a timeline. List examples of styles and types of clothing for each time period. To get ideas, think about your parents' and grandparents' clothes and about the clothes in old movies. Work with a partner.

Time periods	Examples of styles and types of clothing
1. now _____	
2. the 1980s	
3. the 1970s	
4. the 1960s	miniskirts
5. the 1950s	

2 | Active Previewing

Preview the magazine article below. Then answer the following questions with a partner.

1. What is the topic of the text?

2. What is the main idea of the text?

REMEMBER

To preview, read the first sentence of each paragraph. See page 60 for more information on *previewing first sentences.*

A. Read the text. Stop after each paragraph. Tell a partner one thing that you remember about it.

Fashion from the Past: The 80s Look

1 We all notice this: Fashions seem to match ten-year periods, or decades. In fact, people often use a decade to describe a certain style. For example, when we hear "50s styles," we think of skinny neckties and hats for men and full skirts and saddle shoes for women. When we hear "60s styles," we think of the hippy look: blue jeans and flower designs. The "70s" might make us think of platform shoes and tight pants. What about the 80s? Let's take a trip back to the 1980s and look at 80s styles.

2 Here's what young people in the United States and the United Kingdom wore in the 1980s: For women it was tapered jeans, jackets with shoulder pads, and short skirts. For men, it was skinny ties (again!). Bright colors were important for both men and women.

3 **80s Girls**

Curly hairstyles were in[1] for women and girls. If an 80s woman had naturally curly hair, great! If not, she went to the hairdresser and got a permanent, a chemical process to make her hair curly. Brown, navy, and all black were out; instead, bright colors were in. Girls and women wore brightly colored sweatshirts with the collar and sleeves cut off. The movie *Flashdance* inspired this look.

4 With their sweatshirts, girls and women wore tapered blue jeans or short skirts. This look also included jackets with shoulder pads, high-heeled shoes, skinny belts, and cheap jewelry such as plastic hoop earrings. 80s girls who were not shy copied Madonna's daring "Boy-Toy" look: lace gloves, large hair bows, faux (never real!) pearls. To complete the look, they wore blue eye shadow—makeup—on their eyes.

5 **80s Guys**

The TV show *Miami Vice* is a good example of 80s fashion for guys. The 80s guy wore light-

Miami Vice

continued

---

[1] **in:** in style; popular

continued

80s styles for men: parachute pants and loafers without socks

colored jackets—for example, pink or white—with the sleeves rolled up and loafers without socks. The clean-shaved look was out—instead, many guys had a 5 o'clock shadow. Skinny neckties, especially in leather, completed this look.

> **Fashion can be a mirror of the times.**

6   The 80s guy also wore parachute pants. Hip-hop artist MC Hammer helped to make parachute pants popular. If they just wanted to be casual, 80s guys wore their 80s concert T-shirt[2] with their holey jeans[3]. Black Converse All-Stars® or Vans® sneakers were their favorite casual shoes.

7   Fashion can be a mirror of the times. By looking at 80s fashion, we can see that it was a fun and colorful decade in the U.S. and the U.K.

---

[2] **concert T-shirt:** a T-shirt that advertises a rock concert
[3] **holey jeans:** jeans with holes in them

B. Read the text again without stopping. Tell your partner two new pieces of information that you remember.

C. Work as a class or in large groups. Try to name as many things as you can about the text.

4 | Understanding the Topic, Main Idea, and Supporting Details

A. Answer the questions. Write *T* for the *Topic*, MI for *Main Idea*, G for *Too General*, and *S* for *Too Specific*.

1. What is the topic of *Text 2*?

   a. _____ fashion from the past

   b. _____ the "Boy Toy" look

   c. _____ 80s fashion

2. What is the main idea of *Text 2*?

   a. _____ 1980s fashion was fun and colorful.

   b. _____ Fashion reflects the times.

   c. _____ *Flashdance* and *Miami Vice* inspired 1980s fashion.

3. What is the topic of ¶2?

   a. _____ what women wore in the 80s in the U.S. and the U.K.

   b. _____ what young people in the U.S. and the U.K. wore in the 80s

   c. _____ what young people wore in the 80s

4. What is the main idea of ¶5?

   a. _____ Skinny pants and jeans, wide shoulder pads, and bright colors were 80s styles.

   b. _____ Skinny ties and bright colors were styles for men in the 80s.

   c. _____ Young people wore particular styles in the 1980s.

B. Check (✔) the supporting details. Discuss your answers with a partner.

1. What are the two supporting details for the main idea of ¶1?

   ☐ a. "50s styles" makes us think of skinny ties and full skirts.

   ☐ b. Platform shoes are shoes with thick soles.

   ☐ c. "60s styles" makes us think of the hippy look.

2. What are the two supporting details for the main idea of ¶5?

   ☐ a. *Miami Vice* was a popular TV show in the 80s.

   ☐ b. *Miami Vice* inspired the light-colored jackets of the 80s.

   ☐ c. *Miami Vice* inspired the 5 o'clock shadow look of the 80s.

5 | Understanding the Text

A. Write *T* for *True* and *F* for *False* according to the information in the text. Try not to look at the text. Discuss your answers with a partner.

_____ 1. A decade is a ten-year period.

_____ 2. Platform shoes are an example of 50s style.

_____ 3. Big-shouldered jackets are an example of 80s style.

_____ 4. Expensive jewelry was popular in the 80s.

_____ 5. Leather neckties were an 80s style.

B. Complete the chart. Give examples from the text of the following 80s fashion influences. Discuss your answers with a partner.

Fashion influences	Examples
1. *Flashdance*	
2. Madonna	
3. *Miami Vice*	light-colored jackets
4. MC Hammer	

 VOCABULARY STRATEGY Understanding Vocabulary in Context—
Pictures

Pictures in texts can often help you to understand new words. When you see a new word in a text, look for a picture and a caption that might explain it. Sometimes you will find the new word in the caption. Sometimes, you only have a picture. Match the word with the picture to understand its meaning.

Look at ¶5 of *Text 1* on page 115.

You can tell from the context that batik, embroidery, and block printing are traditional types of Thai textile designs, but you might not know exactly what they are. The picture and caption on page 115 help you to understand them because you can see what they look like.

6 | Understanding Vocabulary in Context—Pictures

Explain these 80s styles to your partner. Use the pictures in *Text 2* to help you understand them.

1. tapered jeans (¶2)

2. shoulder pads (¶4)

3. loafers without socks (¶5)

4. parachute pants (¶6)

VOCABULARY STRATEGY Understanding Vocabulary in Context—Contrasts

Another strategy for understanding unfamiliar words is to look for **contrasts**. Contrasts show differences between two words or phrases. When you read sentences with contrasts, you can sometimes understand new words. Contrasts often follow expressions such as *not*, *never*, *instead (of)*, and *unlike*.

Read this sentence:
The clean-shaved look was out—instead, many guys had a *5 o'clock shadow*.

You might not know what *a 5 o'clock shadow* is, but if you understand "clean-shaved" and know that *instead* indicates contrast, then you can guess that a *5 o'clock shadow* probably means "not shaved" or having some hair on the face.

7 | Understanding Vocabulary in Context—Contrasts

Use contrasts in the text to help you write a definition for each of the words and phrases from *Text 2*.

1. were out (¶3) _____

2. daring (¶4) _____

3. faux (¶4) _____

VOCABULARY STRATEGY Understanding Possessive Pronouns

Possessive pronouns are like adjectives because they modify nouns, pronouns, or noun phrases. The *possessive* pronouns are: **my**, **your**, **her**, **his**, **its**, **our**, and **their**. Sometimes, a possessive pronoun refers to a noun, pronoun, or noun phrase in the same sentence. Sometimes, the noun, pronoun, or noun phrase is in another sentence.

Read these sentences:

1. Khun Lee's academic background was in biochemical science, but *her* hobby was clothing design.

Whose hobby was clothing design? Kung Lee's.

2. Khun Lee opened the first Senada Theory store in the Siam Centre in 2002. *Her* second store is in Gaysorn.

Who does *her* refer to in the second sentence? Khun Lee.

8 | Understanding Possessive Pronouns

Write the words that the possessive pronouns refer to in *Text 2*.

1. In ¶3, what does *her* (her hair) refer to? _an 80s woman_

2. In ¶4, what does *their* (their eyes) refer to? _____

3. In ¶6, what do these possessive pronouns refer to?

a. their (their 80s concert T-shirt) _____

b. their (their holey jeans) _____

c. their (their favorite casual shoes) _____

9 | Discussing the Issues

Answer the questions and discuss your answers with a partner.

1. Did anyone in your family wear 80s styles? If yes, what did they wear?

2. Do fashions from the past become popular again? If yes, give examples.

3. What do you think popular fashions of the next decade will look like?

Text 3 | Clothing Costs

1 | Getting Started

Answer the questions and discuss your answers with a partner.

1. How much money do you spend on clothes?

2. Do you think that clothes are too expensive? Why or why not?

2 | Active Previewing

Preview the table on the next page. Then answer the questions. Discuss your answers with a partner.

1. What is the title of the table? _____

2. What words are in the top row? _____

3. Are there any subheadings? _____

4. What is the topic of the table? _____

> **REMEMBER**
>
> Preview the table by looking at the title, especially the important words. Then look at the top-row headings and any subheadings. See page 26 for more information on *understanding and previewing tables*.

Clothing Costs, Then And Now

The following chart shows the amount of money that people spent on clothing in the U.S. at different time periods. It also shows the percentage of all expenditures[1] that went for[2] clothing.

Year	Annual[3] Apparel[4] Expenditures	Percent of Total Expenditures
1901	$107	14.7
1917-1919	$238	17.6
1934-1936	$160	10.9
1950	$435	11.6
1960-1961	$559	10.3
1972-1973	$722	8.4
1986-1987	$1,061	5.2
2000-2003	$1,640	4.0

Note: Amounts are in U.S. Dollars.

[1] **expenditures:** money that people spend

[2] **that went for:** that people spent on

[3] **annual:** each year

[4] **apparel:** clothing

3 | Scanning Tables

Scan the table above to find the answers to the questions. Discuss your answers with a partner.

1. How much money did people spend on clothing on 1901? _____

2. How much money did people spend on clothing in 1950? _____

3. How much money did people spend on clothing during 2000–2003? _____

4. In what year did people pay the greatest percentage of their total expenditures on clothing?

_____

5. In what year did people pay the smallest percentage of their total expenditures on clothing?

_____

4 | Discussing the Issues

Answer the questions and discuss your answers with a partner.

1. Guess: Why might the percentage of total expenditures on clothing be smaller now than it was in the past?

2. What percentage of your total expenditures goes for clothing? Compare your answer with the percentages in the table. Which time period do you match?

3. Do you know some ways to spend less money on clothes? If yes, discuss them with the class.

Text 4 | What Is Fashion?

1 | Getting Started

A. Answer the questions and discuss your answers with a partner.

1. What does fashion mean to you?

2. Is fashion important to you? Why or why not?

3. Where do fashion ideas come from?

B. Look at the clothes you are wearing. Why are you wearing them? Check (✔) the reasons. Discuss your answers with a partner.

My clothes...	Yes	No
1. ...protect me.	☐	☐
2. ...make me attractive.	☐	☐
3. ...show my emotions (how I feel today).	☐	☐
4. ...show a group that I belong to.	☐	☐
5. Other:	☐	☐

 READING SKILL Making Predictions

You can preview a text by **making predictions**—thinking about what the text is about *before* you read it. To make predictions, look at the title and any headings. Look at the pictures and read the captions. These parts of the text tell you the important ideas. Then guess what the author might say about these ideas. Making predictions will help you understand the text better.

2 | Active Previewing

Preview the academic text below. Make predictions. Then discuss the questions with a partner.

1. What is the topic of this text? _____

2. What is the main idea of this text?_____

3. What kind of information will the author probably give? List four things.

_____

3 | Reading and Recalling

A. Read the text. Stop after each paragraph. Tell a partner one thing that you remember about it.

What Is Fashion?

1 We all deal with fashion every day. Some people might say they do not care about clothes. But even these people make fashion decisions. We all choose clothes every morning. Our choices say who we are and how we feel that day.

2 Why Do We Wear Clothes?

There are many important reasons for wearing clothes.

3 • **Protection:** Clothes protect us from cold, rain, and snow. For example, mountain climbers wear high-tech outerwear to stay warm and avoid frostbite.

4 • **Attraction:** Clothes make us attractive to other people. The shape and color of clothes can improve a person's appearance. For example, high-heeled shoes can make a woman look taller, tight shirts can show off a man's muscles, and black makes most people look thinner.

5 • **Emotional expression:** Our clothes show our feelings. We "dress up" when we're happy and "dress down" when we're sad. For example, in many cultures, people wear dark colors to a funeral.

6 • **Identification and tradition:** Our clothes can show the group that we belong to. For example, judges wear robes in court and people in the military wear uniforms. Many

Clothes indicate special occasions and ceremonies.

Orthodox Jewish men wear hats and dark suits and many Islamic women cover their heads. Clothes also indicate special occasions and ceremonies. For example, brides in many cultures wear long white dresses.

7 Where Does Fashion Come From?

We constantly get new fashion ideas from music, books, and television. Movies also have a big impact on fashion. For example, the Ray-

Clothes show the group that we belong to. For example, judges wear robes.

continued

continued

Ban® sunglass company sold more sunglasses after people saw the movie *Men In Black* (1997). Sometimes a fashion style is worldwide. Back in the 1950s, teenagers everywhere dressed like the rock 'n roll star, Elvis Presley.

8   Musicians and movie stars have always influenced fashion, but so have political figures and royalty such as presidents, their spouses, kings, queens, and princesses. For example, Diana, the Princess of Wales, was an important influence on fashion in the 1980s and 1990s. Many women copied her hairstyle and clothes.

9   Popular fashions are almost impossible to trace. For example, no one knows how the short skirts and boots that English teenagers wore in the 1960s got to Paris. No one knows how blue jeans became so popular in the U.S., or how hip-hop styles went from the streets of the Bronx to fashion shows in London and Milan.

Diana, the Princess of Wales, was an important influence on fashion.

10   **Fashion and "High Fashion"**

Fashion is big business. More people are involved in the buying, selling, and making of clothing than any other business in the world. Every day, millions of workers design, sew, glue, dye, and transport clothing to stores.

11   High fashion is defined by the people who have power in the fashion world. Wealthy people, buyers for major department stores, and editors and writers for fashion magazines are all part of Haute Couture ("High Fashion" in French). Some of these expensive and often artistic fashions may become the fashion for the rest of the world. However, most of these fashions never move beyond fashion shows and magazines.

12   **Fashion in History**

People have always read fashion magazines to see the latest styles. In 18th century France, for example, average dressmakers studied sketches of the fashions of the royal court. These drawings showed the latest styles. The dressmakers copied them for their customers. The famous French king Louis XIV said: "Fashion is a mirror." Louis himself was famous for his style. He wore extravagant[1] laces and velvets.

13   Even in the ancient world, fashion was important. Primitive people wore necklaces made from shells. They decorated their clothing with beads and animal teeth. Ancient warriors[2] wore hats with animal bones on them. Rich people in ancient Egypt wore wigs, jewelry, and makeup.

14   James Laver, a costume historian[3], said: "The dress of any given period is exactly suited to[4] the actual climate of the time[5]." When we see tight jeans, we think "the 1980s." Baggy jeans say "the 1990s" and low-cut jeans say "the 2000s."

15   In fact, as the climate of the times changes, so do the fashions. The key word in fashion is change.

---

[1] **extravagant:** exaggerated; overdone

[2] **warrior:** fighter

[3] **a costume historian:** a person who studies clothing from the past to the present

[4] **is...suited to:** is correct or appropriate for

[5] **climate of the time:** the way the world is at a particular time

B. Read the text again without stopping. Tell your partner two new pieces of information that you remember.

C. Work as a class or in large groups. Try to say as many things as you can about the text.

4 | Understanding the Topic, Main Idea, and Supporting Details

A. Answer the questions or write _T_ for the _Topic_, _MI_ for _Main Idea_, _G_ for _Too General_, and _S_ for _Too Specific_.

1. What is the topic of _Text 4_? _____

2. What is the main idea of _Text 4_? _____

3. What is the topic of ¶**4**?

    a. _____ wearing clothes to be attractive

    b. _____ why people wear high-heeled shoes

    c. _____ why people wear clothes

4. What is the main idea of ¶**4**?

    a. _____ People wear clothes for many reasons.

    b. _____ One reason people wear clothes is to look thinner.

    c. _____ One reason people wear clothes is to be attractive to others.

B. Check (✔) the supporting details. Discuss your answers with a partner.

1. What are the two supporting details for the main idea of ¶**7**?

    ☐ a. The Ray-Ban® company sold more sunglasses because of the movie _Men in Black_.

    ☐ b. Elvis Presley was popular everywhere in the world.

    ☐ c. In the 1950s, teenagers everywhere dressed like Elvis Presley.

2. What are the two supporting details for the main idea of ¶**13**?

    ☐ a. Ancient warriors killed animals.

    ☐ b. Primitive people wore necklaces made from shells.

    ☐ c. Rich Egyptians wore jewelry.

5 | Understanding the Text

A. Answer as many questions as you can without looking at _Text 4_. Discuss your answers with a partner.

1. Why do people wear clothes? Give at least two reasons. _____

    _____

2. Where does fashion come from? Give at least two examples. _____

    _____

3. Who decides what "high fashion" is? _____

4. What is one example of an ancient "fashion"? _____

B. Write *T* for *True* and *F* for *False* according to the information in the text. Try not to look at the text. Discuss your answers with a partner.

_____ **1.** A judge wearing a robe is an example of wearing clothes to show a special occasion.

_____ **2.** Princess Diana is an example of how royalty can influence fashion.

_____ **3.** Popular fashions are easy to trace.

_____ **4.** More people work in the clothing business than any other business in the world.

_____ **5.** Ancient people were not concerned about fashion.

6 | Understanding Vocabulary in Context—Collocations

Select the best meaning for each collocation according to *Text 4*.

1. show off (¶4)

    a. hide   b. make to look good   c. improve

2. dress up (¶5)

    a. wear dark clothes   b. wear colorful clothes   c. wear nice clothes

3. have a(n)…impact on (¶7)

    a. influence   b. ignore   c. sell

> **REMEMBER**
>
> Collocations are groups of words that often appear together. See page 110 for more on *collocations*.

7 | Discussing the Issues

Answer the questions and discuss your answers with a partner.

1. Explain James Laver's quote in ¶14. Give examples of current styles that "are suited to the climate of the time."

2. What current styles might still be popular in the future?

Putting It On Paper

A. Write a paragraph on one of these topics.

1. Describe your favorite piece of clothing. Explain why it is your favorite.

2. Explain how current fashions are suited to life in the world today.

Steps for your paragraph

a. State the main idea of your paragraph in the first sentence. This is your topic sentence.

b. Include in your paragraph three supporting details that explain your idea. Use facts, opinions, statistics, and/or examples.

c. Try to use words and expressions from this chapter.

B. Exchange paragraphs with a partner. Read your partner's paragraph. Answer the questions in the checklist. Give feedback to your partner.

✔ CHECKLIST
1. Is there a clear main idea?
2. Are there enough supporting details? What types of supporting details are they?
3. Do all the supporting details connect to the main idea?
4. Are there words and expressions from this chapter?
5. Write additional comments below.

_____

_____

_____

_____

_____

_____

_____

_____

_____

_____

C. Use your partner's feedback to revise your work.

Taking It Online | Exploring Fashion

A. With a partner, use the Internet to find information about the history of a fashion.

1. Choose a fashion that interests you. It can be clothing (for example, neckties, shoes, or jeans), hairstyles or facial hair (for example, wigs, long hair on men, or beards), jewelry, or makeup. Find out as much as you can about the history of the fashion. Bring pictures of your fashion to class.

2. Use Google (www.google.com) or another major search engine to find sites with the information you want.

3. Preview the sites as you would a magazine article.

ONLINE TIP

Go to Google Images to find pictures of your fashion. Combine key words, just as with a regular search—for example: "wig ancient Egypt." Save pictures "to disk" to print later.

B. Complete the table with the information you find.

Fashion
Type of fashion:
Name of Website:
Website address:
When did people first wear the fashion? Where did they wear it?
What or who influenced the fashion?
How is/was the fashion "suited to the climate of the times"?
Has the fashion changed over time? How?
Other facts:

C. Following up. Share your facts with your classmates. Which fashion is the oldest? Which fashion is the strangest? Which fashion is the most attractive? Which fashion do people still wear? Which fashion would you wear?

Chapter 8

Ethics in Education

READING SKILLS

- Reviewing Reading Skills

VOCABULARY STRATEGIES

- Reviewing Vocabulary Strategies

GRAPHICS

- Previewing Flowcharts, page 142
- Scanning Flowcharts, page 143

Answer the questions and discuss your answers with a partner.

1. Do you ever help your classmates with their schoolwork? If yes, give examples.

2. Look at the photos. What are the people doing?

3. What parts of being a student are easy for you? What parts are difficult for you?

Text 1 | What Is Cheating?

1 | Getting Started

A. Answer the questions and discuss your answers with a partner.

1. What is the meaning of *cheating*?

2. Is the meaning of *cheating* the same everywhere in the world? Give examples to support your answer. If you aren't sure, guess.

B. Give examples of cheating. Complete the chart. Discuss your chart with a partner.

Situations	Examples of cheating
1. At home	
2. At work	
3. At school	

2 | Active Previewing

Preview the magazine quiz on the next page. Then answer the following questions with a partner.

1. What is the topic of this quiz?

2. What kind of information will it have?

3 | Reading and Recalling

A. Read the text. Stop after each paragraph. Circle your answer. Try not to read the correct answers until after you take the quiz.

> **REMEMBER**
> Underlining the important words in the title can help you preview a text. Look at the pictures and captions. Make predictions. See page 47 for more information on *making predictions*.

That's Cheating! (Or Is It?)

Read the following situations. Circle "Cheating" if the behavior is not OK and "OK" if the behavior is OK.

1. You have to write a difficult essay. Your friend is a better writer. Is it OK to ask your friend to write it for you, but put your own name on it?

   Cheating   OK

2. You find an article on the Internet. It's on the topic of your essay. Is it OK to copy a paragraph and put it into your essay?

   Cheating   OK

3. You find an interview with an expert. Her words are perfect for your essay. Is it OK to use her words if you put quotation marks (" ") around them?

   Cheating   OK

4. You are taking a test. The person next to you copies your answers. Is it OK to tell the teacher?

   Cheating   OK

> **Is it OK to copy a paragraph and put it into your essay?**

5. You are a good test-taker. A friend asks you to take the TOEFL exam for her. Is it OK for you to take the test for her?

   Cheating   OK

6. You read many books and articles to get ideas for an essay. You use many of the ideas from your reading. You don't exactly remember where you got each idea. Is it OK to pretend that the ideas are your own when you write your essay?

   Cheating   OK

7. You and a friend study together before a big test. Your friend knows some important things that you don't know. He helps you to remember these things for the test. Is this OK?

   Cheating   OK

8. You and a friend have to write an essay on the same topic. You write your essays separately, but you check each other's papers and make corrections before you hand them in. Is this OK?

   Cheating   OK

Is it OK to tell the teacher when someone copies your answers?

Is it OK to take the TOEFL for your friend?

Is it OK to check a friend's paper for grammar mistakes?

Correct Answers

In North American academic culture, the following answers are correct:
Cheating: 1, 2, 5, 6 OK: 3. But include her name, too; 4. This helps everyone in the class; 7. In fact, this is a very good idea!; 8. This is also a good idea.

B. Read the text again without stopping. Tell your partner two new pieces of information that you remember.

C. Work as a class or in large groups. Try to say as many things as you can about the text.

4 | Understanding the Topic and the Main Idea

Answer the questions. Write *T* for the *Topic*, *MI* for *Main Idea*, *G* for *Too General*, and *S* for *Too Specific*.

1. What is the topic of *Text 1*?

    a. _____ copying from the Internet in North American academic culture

    b. _____ cheating in North American academic culture

    c. _____ what is cheating and what isn't cheating in North American academic culture

2. What is the main idea of *Text 1*?

    a. _____ There are rules for correct academic behavior in North America.

    b. _____ Taking a test for someone else is cheating in North American academic culture.

    c. _____ There are rules for correct academic behavior.

5 | Understanding the Text

A. Write *T* for *True* and *F* for *False* according to the information in the text. Try not to look at the text. Discuss your answers with a partner.

_____ 1. It's OK to ask a friend to write an essay for you, as long as you put your name on it.

_____ 2. If you use someone else's words, you should put quotation marks around them.

_____ 3. In North American academic culture, it's cheating to take an exam for someone else.

_____ 4. It's OK to help a friend edit his or her essay.

_____ 5. In North American academic culture, it's not OK to help a friend study for a test.

B. Take the quiz again. Try not to look at the answers. Did you get all correct answers this time?

6 | Understanding Subject, Object, and Possessive Pronouns

Write the word or phrase that each pronoun refers to in *Text 1*.

1. Your (Your friend) (**Q2**) _____

2. Her (Her words) (**Q3**) _____

3. her (for her) (**Q5**) _____

4. He (He helps) (**Q7**) _____

5. them (hand them in) (**Q8**) _____

7 | Discussing the Issues

Answer the questions and discuss your answers with a partner.

1. Did any of the rules of North American academic behavior surprise you? If yes, which ones?

2. Are the rules of North American academic behavior different from academic behavior rules in another country or culture that you know? If yes, explain.

3. Describe your experiences with cheating in school situations.

Text 2 | Plagiarism

1 | Getting Started

A. Answer the questions and discuss your answers with a partner.

1. Do you like writing essays? Why or why not?

2. When you write an essay, where do you usually get your ideas?

B. Check (✔) the good sources of information. Explain to a partner how you could use your checked items to write an essay.

- [ ] **1.** a TV show
- [ ] **2.** a movie
- [ ] **3.** a magazine article
- [ ] **4.** a website
- [ ] **5.** an advertisement
- [ ] **6.** a song
- [ ] **7.** an interview
- [ ] **8.** your own emails

> **REMEMBER**
>
> Combining strategies helps you read more quickly and understand and remember important ideas. See page 148 for more on *combining strategies*.

2 | Active Previewing

Preview the online article below. Then answer the following questions with a partner.

1. What is the topic of the text? _____

2. What is the main idea of the text? _____

3. What kind of information will the author give? List two things.

_____

REMEMBER

To preview, look at the important words in the title. Read the headings. Read the first sentence of each paragraph. Make predictions. See page 47 for more information on *making predictions*.

3 | Reading and Recalling

A. Read the text. Stop after each paragraph. Tell a partner one thing that you remember about it.

Avoiding Plagiarism

1　Plagiarism means using somebody else's words or ideas without giving that person credit[1]. Plagiarism is not allowed at North American schools, including elementary schools, high schools, colleges, and universities. Plagiarism is sometimes intentional, but it can also be accidental. American schools punish both types. For example, schools often ask students who commit plagiarism[2] to leave. It's a big problem today because the Internet makes it easy to find articles and copy them. It's easy to copy something by accident, so it's very important to know how to avoid plagiarism. Citing sources—giving credit—is the best way to avoid plagiarism. Here are some tips from Purdue University for citing sources.

2　**Knowing When to Cite Sources**
Sometimes you need to give credit to other people's ideas; sometimes you don't. How do you know?

3　You need to cite sources when:
- You are using somebody else's words or ideas from any source, including magazines, books, newspapers, songs, TV programs, movies, web pages, computer programs, letters, or advertisements.
- You copy exact words from anywhere.
- You use someone else's diagrams, illustrations, charts, or pictures.
- You use ideas that you got from other people in an interview, a conversation, or an e-mail.

continued

---

[1] **giving...credit:** stating where (or from whom) you found words or ideas
[2] **commit plagiarism:** do something that is considered plagiarism

4   You do not need to cite sources when:
  • You are writing about your own experiences, your own observations[3], your own thoughts, or your own ideas about a subject.
  • You are using "common knowledge"—for example, folklore, common sense observations ("the sun rises in the east"), or shared information within your field of study or your culture.
  • You are writing about generally accepted facts—for example, the laws of science.
  • You are writing the results of your own experiments.

5   **Making Sure That You Are Safe**
     Purdue University has many suggestions for avoiding plagiarism during the writing process. Here are some of them.

6   When you are doing research for a paper:
  • Mark everything in your notes that uses someone else's words a big Q (for quote) or with big quotation marks.
  • Mark ideas that are from sources with an S. Mark your own ideas with ME.
  • Make notes on all of the source information—including the authors, titles, page numbers, and dates of your source material. Do not wait until later to find this information.

7   When you quote:
  • Mention the person's name either at the beginning of the quote, or at the end.
  • Put quotation marks around the words that you are quoting; for example: James Laver, a costume historian said, "The dress of any given period is exactly suited to the actual climate of the time."

8   No one wants to plagiarize intentionally, and if you follow these guidelines, you'll probably avoid accidental plagiarism, too.

---

[3] **your...observations:** things that you see or notice

B. Read the text again without stopping. Tell your partner two new pieces of information that you remember.

C. Work as a class or in large groups. Try to say as many things as you can about the text.

4 | Understanding the Topic, Main Idea, and Supporting Details

A. Answer the questions. Write *T* for the *Topic*, *MI* for *Main Idea*, *G* for *Too General*, and *S* for *Too Specific*.

1. What is the topic of *Text 2*?

   a. _____ plagiarism

   b. _____ how to avoid plagiarism

   c. _____ citing sources

2. What is the main idea of *Text 2*?

   a. _____ You need to cite sources when you use somebody else's words.

   b. _____ It's important to avoid plagiarism.

   c. _____ There are things that you can do to avoid plagiarism.

3. What is the topic of ¶3?

   a. _____ citing sources

   b. _____ when to cite sources

   c. _____ citing sources when you use someone else's ideas

4. What is the main idea of ¶6?

   a. _____ There are things you can do to avoid plagiarism during the research process.

   b. _____ During the writing process, you should mark your own ideas with "ME."

   c. _____ There are things you can do to avoid plagiarism.

B. Check (✔) the supporting details. Discuss your answers with a partner.

1. What are the two supporting details for the main idea of ¶3?

   ☐ a. Cite sources when you copy exact words.

   ☐ b. TV programs are considered sources.

   ☐ c. Cite sources when you use ideas from a conversation, interview, or e-mail.

2. What are the two supporting details for the main idea of ¶6?

   ☐ a. "ME" means my ideas.

   ☐ b. Mark everything that is someone else's ideas with a Q.

   ☐ c. Make notes on all your source information.

5 | Understanding the Text

A. Answer as many questions as you can without looking at the text. Discuss your answers with a partner.

1. What happens in a North American school if you commit plagiarism?

_____

2. Why is plagiarism a big problem today? _____

3. When do you need to cite sources? Give one example. _____

4. When do you *not* need to cite sources? Give one example. _____

5. What can you do to avoid plagiarism when you are doing research for a paper? Give one example. _____

6. How do you quote other people's words? Rewrite the following to show the correct way: The only -ism Hollywood believes in is plagiarism. —Dorothy Parker, American writer.

_____

B. Read the situations. Write *C* if you need to cite a source; write *NC* if you do not need to cite a source. There may be two answers for some situations.

_____ 1. You interviewed your grandmother for an essay on 1960s fashions.

_____ 2. You are going to write a review of a movie. You didn't have time to see the movie, but you found a good review of it in the newspaper.

_____ 3. You wrote a story for your English class about something that happened in your hometown when you were a child. You are going to use a photograph of your hometown in your paper. You found it on the Internet.

_____ 4. You did an experiment: You compared two types of chemicals for your chemistry class. You are going to write about what happened in the experiment.

_____ 5. You are going to write a paper about personal distance for an anthropology class. You didn't have time to read any books, but you saw a TV program about personal distance. You will use ideas from the TV show in your paper.

6 | Understanding Vocabulary in Context—Definitions, Examples, and Contrasts

Read the following sentences from *Text 2*. Check (✔) the part of speech for the underlined words and expressions. Then write their meanings on the lines.

1. Plagiarism means using somebody else's words or ideas without giving that person credit.

☐ a. noun   ☐ b. verb   ☐ c. adjective

_____

2. Plagiarism is sometimes intentional, but it can also be accidental.

☐ a. noun   ☐ b. verb   ☐ c. adjective

_____

3. American schools punish both types. For example, schools often ask students who commit plagiarism to leave.

☐ a. noun   ☐ b. verb   ☐ c. adjective

_____

4. Citing sources—giving credit—is the best way to avoid plagiarism.

☐ a. noun   ☐ b. verb   ☐ c. adjective

_____

7 | Understanding Vocabulary in Context—Collocations

Select the best meaning for each collocation according to the text.

1. common knowledge (¶4)

    a. observations that you have made yourself

    b. things that everyone knows

    c. results of experiments

2. generally accepted facts (¶4)

    a. folktales that everyone knows

    b. facts that you believe to be true

    c. facts that everyone agrees are true

8 | Discussing the Issues

Answer the questions and discuss your answers with a partner.

1. Did any of the information in *Text 2* surprise you? If yes, give examples.

2. Do you think the rules for citing sources in *Text 2* are the same everywhere in the world? Give examples to support your answer.

3. Do you have any ideas for avoiding plagiarism? If yes, share them with the class.

Text 3 | Citing Sources

1 | Getting Started

Discuss your answers with a partner.

1. How do you write an essay? Describe the steps.

2. What decisions do you have to make when you write an essay?

 GRAPHICS Previewing Flowcharts

Flowcharts are diagrams that show steps in a process. They show the steps in a combination of words and graphics. The words usually appear inside squares, rectangles, diamonds, circles, and other shapes. The words inside diamonds and circles usually show decisions you can make about the situations. These are decision points. Arrows connect situations with decision points. To **preview** a flowchart, first read the title. Then look at the whole flowchart at once. Look at the size of the flowchart and the number of decision points—the diamonds and circles. This will give you an idea of how many steps there are in the process.

2 | Previewing Flowcharts

Preview the flowchart below. Read the title and look at the size of the flowchart. Then answer these questions with a partner.

1. What is the title of the flowchart?

2. How many steps are in the process?

3. How many decision points are in the process?

4. What is the topic of the flowchart?

 GRAPHICS Scanning Flowcharts

When you **scan** a flowchart, quickly read the words inside the squares and rectangles. You can often skip the words in the Yes/No decision points because the shapes indicate the words *Yes* and *No*.

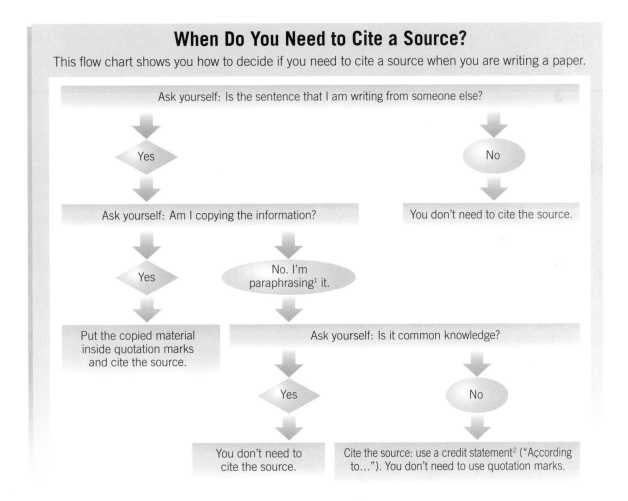

When Do You Need to Cite a Source?

This flow chart shows you how to decide if you need to cite a source when you are writing a paper.

Ask yourself: Is the sentence that I am writing from someone else?

Yes

No

Ask yourself: Am I copying the information?

You don't need to cite the source.

Yes

No. I'm paraphrasing[1] it.

Put the copied material inside quotation marks and cite the source.

Ask yourself: Is it common knowledge?

Yes

No

You don't need to cite the source.

Cite the source: use a credit statement[2] ("According to..."). You don't need to use quotation marks.

---

[1] **paraphrasing:** saying or rewriting something in your own words

[2] **a credit statement:** a phrase that introduces a quotation: According to J. Laver, clothing can tell us a lot about the climate of the time.

3 | Scanning Flowcharts

Scan the flowchart on page 143 to find the answers to the questions. Discuss your answers with a partner.

1. What should you do if you are copying a sentence that contains information from someone else?

   _____

2. What should you ask yourself if you are paraphrasing someone else's information?

   _____

3. What should you do if you are paraphrasing information that is common knowledge?

   _____

4. What should you do if you are using your own words to express someone else's idea?

   _____

4 | Discussing the Issues

Answer the questions and discuss your answers with a partner.

1. The flowchart includes an example of a credit statement: "According to." Another example is "X said." Think of more credit statements that you can use when you quote in an essay.

2. Think of another process such as deciding what to eat or deciding what to wear each day. Make a flowchart to show the process. Share the flowchart with the class.

Text 4 | Cheating with Technology

1 | Getting Started

A. Answer the questions and discuss your answers with a partner.

1. Did you ever think about committing plagiarism? Did you decide not to do it? Why?

2. Give your opinion: Is it possible to commit plagiarism without someone knowing? If yes, how easy or difficult might it be?

3. What might be some ways to learn if people are plagiarizing?

B. Check (✔) the organizations that might worry about plagiarism. Compare your answers with a partner's. Then discuss this question: Why would plagiarism be a problem in these organizations?

- [ ] 1. a newspaper
- [ ] 2. a university
- [ ] 3. a movie-making company
- [ ] 4. a publishing company
- [ ] 5. the United Nations
- [ ] 6. a law firm

2 | Active Previewing

Preview the magazine article below. Then answer the questions with a partner.

1. What is the topic of this text? _____

2. What is the main idea of this text? _____

3. What kind of information will the author probably give? List four things.

_____

_____

REMEMBER

To preview, look at the important words in the title. Read the headings. Read the first sentence of each paragraph. Make predictions. See page 47 for more information on *making predictions*.

3 | Reading and Recalling

A. Read the text. Stop after each paragraph. Tell a partner one thing that you remember about it.

Plagiarism Software

1 Plagiarism is a growing problem. Recently, researchers did a survey of 30,000 students at 34 colleges. Thirty-seven percent of the students in the survey said that they committed plagiarism. The most common type of plagiarism was copying material from the Internet. Internet plagiarism isn't only a problem at schools and universities. Many businesses—for example, newspapers—have problems with this type of plagiarism. As a result, companies are providing software and services that detect[1] plagiarism, and these companies have many customers.

How Does It Work?

2 Most people commit Internet plagiarism by changing words or adding sentences to the original article. Plagiarism software can often find these changes and additions. This software can check billions of digital documents[2] and find similarities and differences in just seconds.

3 Here's one way to detect plagiarism: A com-

> Most people commit Internet plagiarism by changing words or adding sentences to the original article.

pany buys a software program. They use the program to compare a new document—for example, a student's essay or a draft of a magazine article—to existing documents. This software analyzes the new document. It makes a kind of map of the document. This is called a "digital fingerprint." Then the program compares the fingerprint of the new document with material on the Internet.

4 Another type of product is web-based. A user such as a teacher, subscribes to[3] a service and then uploads documents—these are often student papers—to a website. The service searches the Internet for any documents that are similar to the uploaded papers. The service then sends a report to the user. The report describes the similarities between the student papers and other material on the Internet. These services can search through millions of web pages a day.

Who Uses It?

5 Law firms and even the United Nations are using plagiarism-detection software and services. Most of these organizations do not talk about pla-

continued

---

[1] **detect:** find

[2] **digital documents:** electronic documents; documents that are on a computer or a website

[3] **subscribes to:** pays money for

continued

giarism detecting. They ask the software makers and service providers not to discuss their clients. Why? It's bad publicity. Companies usually don't want the public to hear about their plagiarizing authors, employees, or consultants. Here's an example: A publishing company hired a plagiarism-detecting company. They were concerned about an author. They thought he might be plagiarizing. Their fears were correct—the author, a famous textbook author—was indeed plagiarizing other sources. The publishing company quietly fixed the author's work and no one ever heard about it. The author kept his good reputation[4].

6   The president of the plagiarism detection company said: "I see a lot of plagiarism every day. Most authors—whether a student or a professional author—think that no one will catch them. They think that cheating is worth the risk."

7   This same company also helped a major newspaper. A local university president wrote an article for the newspaper. A reader notified the newspaper that some of the sentences in the article looked familiar. The newspaper used the company's plagiarism-detecting software. The software showed this: The article included material from four sources, including *The New York* *Times*. It found that eleven percent of the university president's article was not original.

8   **Why Not Use It?**

Plagiarism detectors are relatively inexpensive. However, many companies do not use them. Why? Some companies are afraid of lawsuits. They are afraid that if they accuse[5] someone of plagiarism, the person will take them to court. Also, not everyone agrees on the definition of plagiarism. For example, what percentage of copied material in a document makes it plagiarized? Is detection software always accurate? These issues are still unclear.

9   **Is It Worth It?**

Many plagiarists work hard to hide their plagiarism: They change words, add new material, and reorganize sentences or sections of the original material. It can be just as much work to plagiarize as it is to write something original. Since many schools and companies use plagiarism detection, they often catch plagiarists. So is plagiarism worth it? Most people agree: Plagiarism isn't worth the time that it takes and the trouble that it can cause.

---

[4] **reputation:** the public opinion of a person
[5] **accuse:** state that someone has done something wrong

B. Read the text again without stopping. Tell your partner two new pieces of information that you remember.

C. Work as a class or in large groups. Try to say as many things as you can about the text.

4 | Understanding the Topic, Main Idea, and Supporting Details

A. Answer the questions or write *T* for the *Topic*, *MI* for *Main Idea*, *G* for *Too General*, and *S* for *Too Specific*.

1. What is the topic of *Text 4*? _____

2. What is the main idea of *Text 4*? _____

3. What is the topic of ¶**3**?

    a. _____ how plagiarism-detecting software analyzes a document

    b. _____ ways to detect plagiarism

    c. _____ how plagiarism-detecting software works

4. What is the main idea of ¶**5**?

    a. _____ All kinds of organizations use plagiarism-detecting software.

    b. _____ The United Nations uses plagiarism-detecting software.

    c. _____ Many organizations use plagiarism-detecting software, but they do not talk about it.

5. What is the topic of ¶**4**? _____

6. What is the main idea of ¶**4**? _____

B. Check (✔) the supporting details. Answer the questions. Discuss your answers with a partner.

1. What are the two supporting details for the main idea of ¶**5**?

    ☐ a. Organizations ask plagiarism-detecting software companies not to talk about their customers.

    ☐ b. Organizations do not want the public to know that they have plagiarizing employees.

    ☐ c. Some important organizations have employees that commit plagiarism.

2. What are two supporting details in ¶**9**?

_____

_____

5 | Understanding the Text

A. Answer as many questions as you can without looking at the text. Discuss your answers with a partner.

1. What is the most common type of plagiarism? _____

2. How does plagiarism-detecting software work? _____

3. What kinds of organizations use plagiarism-detecting software? Give two examples.

_____

4. Why do organizations tell plagiarism-detecting software companies not to talk about their customers? _____

5. What is one reason not to use plagiarism-detecting software? _____

B. Write *T* for *True* and *F* for *False* according to the information in the text. Try not to look at the text. Discuss your answers with a partner.

_____ **1.** About one-third of students in a survey said that they commit plagiarism.

_____ **2.** Most people commit Internet plagiarism by copying original web articles without making any changes.

_____ **3.** A famous textbook author committed plagiarism but his company did not punish him.

_____ **4.** Plagiarism-detecting software is expensive.

_____ **5.** Most people agree on the definition of "plagiarism."

Good readers put different vocabulary strategies together as they read. They guess the meanings of new words and collocations. They think about the meanings of pronouns. In other words, they **combine vocabulary strategies**. Combining strategies helps you to read more quickly and understand your reading better.

6 | Understanding Vocabulary in Context—Combining Strategies

Guess the meanings of the underlined words and expressions in *Text 4*. Write your guesses on the lines.

1. This software <u>analyzes</u> the new document. It makes a kind of map of the document. This is called a "<u>digital fingerprint</u>." Then the program compares the fingerprint of the new document with material on the Internet. _____

2. It's bad <u>publicity</u>. Companies usually don't want the public to hear about their plagiarizing authors, employees, or consultants. _____

3. Most authors—whether a student or a professional author—think that no one will catch them. They think that cheating is <u>worth the risk</u>. _____

4. Some companies are afraid of <u>lawsuits</u>. They are afraid that if they accuse someone of plagiarism, the person will take them to court. _____

7 | Understanding Subject, Object, and Possessive Pronouns

Write the word or phrase that each pronoun refers to in *Text 4*.

1. It (It makes) (¶3) _____

2. They (They ask) (¶5) _____

3. Their (Their fears) (¶5) _____

4. it (about it) (¶5) _____

5. his (his good reputation) (¶5) _____

8 | Discussing the Issues

Answer the questions and discuss your answers with a partner.

1. Why might each of these people try to commit plagiarism: a student, a university president who is writing an article, and a famous textbook author?

2. Some students commit plagiarism because they are under pressure; that is, they do not have enough time to do their own work. What are some ways that a student can avoid pressure?

Putting It On Paper

A. Write a paragraph on one of these topics.

1. Does "cheating" have the same meaning in all cultures? Support your answer with examples.

2. Is plagiarism ever worth it? Why or why not?

Steps for your paragraph

    a. State the main idea of your paragraph in the first sentence. This is your topic sentence.

    b. Include in your paragraph three supporting details that explain your idea. Use facts, opinions, statistics, and/or examples.

    c. Try to use words and expressions from this chapter.

B. Exchange paragraphs with a partner. Read your partner's paragraph. Answer the questions in the checklist. Give feedback to your partner.

✔ CHECKLIST	
	1. Is there a clear main idea?
	2. Are there enough supporting details? What types of supporting details are they?
	3. Do all the supporting details connect to the main idea?
	4. Are there words and expressions from this chapter?
	5. Write additional comments below.

_____

_____

_____

_____

_____

_____

_____

_____

_____

C. Use your partner's feedback to revise your work.

Taking It Online | Cheating and Plagiarism

A. With a partner, use the Internet to find information on college websites about cheating and plagiarism.

ONLINE TIP

College and university websites contain a lot of information. They usually have their own search engines. These search engines will help you to save time when you look for information on their websites.

1. Choose a college or university in an English-speaking country. Some examples are: Diablo Valley College (Pleasant Hill, CA, USA); Western Washington University (Bellingham, WA, USA); University of Toronto (Toronto, Canada); University of Auckland (Auckland, New Zealand). What kind of information does the college or university have on cheating and plagiarism? Do they tell you how to avoid it? Do they tell about the punishment for committing it?

2. Use Google (www.google.com) or another major search engine to find the college or university's website. Put its name into the search box. Then use the college or university's own search engine to find information on cheating and plagiarism. Try the following key words: cheating, plagiarism; plagiarism policy; academic misconduct (behavior that is not correct).

3. Preview the sites as you would a magazine article.

B. Complete the table with the information you find.

College or University
Name of college or university:
Name of Website:
Website address:
Does the website explain how to avoid cheating and plagiarism? If yes, give examples.
Is there information about plagiarism/committing plagiarism? If yes, what is the punishment?
What other information does the website have on cheating and plagiarism?
Other facts:

C. Following up. Share your facts with your classmates. Compare the information colleges and universities have on avoiding cheating and plagiarism. Which website has the most helpful information? What new information did you learn?

Vocabulary Index

Skills and Strategies Index

Reading Skills

Making Predictions, 47, 56, 61, 68, 81,

Previewing
Articles, **2,** 6, 11, 19, 23, 30, 36, 39, 47, 56, 61, 68, 77, 81, 88, 96, 100, 114, 118, 127, 134, 138, 145
Diagrams, **104**
First Sentences, **60,** 68
Flowcharts, **142,** 143
Pictures and Captions, **76,** 77
Tables, **26,** 43, 66, 86, 124

Scanning, 8, 9, 27, 28, 44, 66, 87, 105, 125, 143, 144

Skimming, 106

Understanding
Main Idea, **70,** 71, 79, 84, 85, 90, 98, 102, 108, 116, 121, 129, 136, 140, 146, 147
Paragraph Topics and Main Ideas, **84**
Supporting Details, **91,** 92, 108, 121, 129, 140, 146, 147
Timelines, **8,** 9
Topic, **41,** 42, 49, 58, 62, 71, 79, 84, 90, 98, 102, 108, 116, 121, 129, 136, 140, 146, 147

Vocabulary Strategies

Skipping Words, 5, 11, 19, 22, 39

Understanding
Object Pronouns, **80,** 99, 137, 148
Possessive Pronouns, **123,** 124, 137, 148
Subject Pronouns, **42,** 65, 72, 85, 137, 148
Vocabulary in Context
Collocations, **110,** 130, 142
Combining Strategies, **148**
Contrasts, **123,** 141
Definitions, **51,** 52, 64, 72, 92, 103, 117, 141
Examples, **59,** 65, 85, 92, 117, 141
Pictures, **122**
Synonyms, **24,** 29, 64, 92, 117